British History in Perspective
General Editor: Jeremy Black

PUBLISHED TITLES

D1634838

William Stafford *John Stuart Mill*
Robert Stewart *Party and Politics, 1830–1852*
Bruce Webster *Medieval Scotland*
Ann Williams *Kingship and Government in Pre-Conquest England*
John W. Young *Britain and European Unity, 1945–92*
Michael B. Young *Charles I*

Please note that a sister series, *Social History in Perspective*, is now available.
It covers the key topics in social, cultural and religious history.

British History in Perspective
Series Standing Order
ISBN 0–333–71356–7 hardcover
ISBN 0–333–69331–0 paperback
(*outside North America only*)

You can receive future titles in this series as they are published by placing a
standing order. Please contact your bookseller or, in case of difficulty, write to us
at the address below with your name and address, the title of the series and the
ISBN quoted above.

Customer Services Department, Macmillan Distribution Ltd
Houndmills, Basingstoke, Hampshire RG21 6XS, England

GLADSTONE

Eugenio F. Biagini

First published in Great Britain 2000 by
MACMILLAN PRESS LTD
Houndmills, Basingstoke, Hampshire RG21 6XS and London
Companies and representatives throughout the world

A catalogue record for this book is available from the British Library.

ISBN 0–333–61352–X hardcover
ISBN 0–333–61353–8 paperback

First published in the United States of America 2000 by
ST. MARTIN'S PRESS, INC.,
Scholarly and Reference Division,
175 Fifth Avenue, New York, N.Y. 10010

ISBN 0–312–22738–8

Library of Congress Cataloging-in-Publication Data
Biagini, Eugenio F.
Gladstone / Eugenio F. Biagini
    p.   cm. — (British history in perspective)
Includes bibliographical references and index.
ISBN 0–312–22738–8 (cloth)
1. Gladstone, W. E. (William Ewart), 1809–1898.   2. Great Britain–
–Politics and government—1837–1901.   I. Title.   II. Series.
DA563.4.B48   1999
941.081'092—dc21
[B]   99–22262
                                                              CIP

This book is printed on paper suitable for recycling and made from fully managed and
sustained forest sources.

10   9   8   7   6   5   4   3   2   1
09   08   07   06   05   04   03   02   01   00

Printed in Hong Kong

Für meine Freundin und Geistesverwandte, Almut

CONTENTS

ACKNOWLEDGEMENTS

I wish to thank the Pew Evangelical Scholars Program for supporting the research on which this publication is based. Moreover, I am very grateful to Derek Beales and Peter Clarke for reading and commenting on earlier drafts of this book, which is greatly improved as a result.

INTRODUCTION

'Truth, justice, order, peace, honour, duty, liberty, piety', these are the objects before me in my daily prayers with reference to my public function, which for the present commands (and I fear damages) every other: but this is the best part of me. All the rest is summed up in 'miserere'.[1]

This meditation from Gladstone's diary captures both his self-perception as he was approaching the apex of his powers and career, and the motivations and some of the tensions which make his life so unique and fascinating. Born in 1809, first elected an MP in 1832, he was to be returned by various constituencies in England and Scotland till 1895, when he finally retired from public life. Four times Prime Minister and the most influential Chancellor of the Exchequer of the nineteenth century, he presided over the shaping of the Victorian 'liberal consensus', which was based on free trade and the gradual incorporation into the British 'constitution' of those classes and groups originating from the Industrial Revolution, including the organized labour movement. By the mid-1880s even other sections of the working poor – such as the Welsh and Irish peasants and Scottish crofters, whose communities had traditionally been relegated to the margins of social and economic life in the United Kingdom – fully entered the mainstream of constitutional politics through Gladstone's Liberal party and its ally, Parnell's National party.

Gladstone's political career covered the period of Britain's greatest power and international influence: he began his career as an executive politician in a government which included the Duke of Wellington, who had defeated Napoleon in 1815, and ended it as the premier of another which included H. H. Asquith, who was to lead Britain in the First World War. His name was to become synonymous with classical liberalism not only in Britain, but throughout the British Empire and western

Europe. He was admired and emulated by statesmen in Canada, New Zealand and Australia, as well as by Irish and Indian national spokesmen. In Japan, in the 1880s, prime minister Ito Himbumi was sometimes described as his country's Gladstone (though Ito was rather an admirer of Bismarck's). Italian and German liberals looked up to him as a model, while Bismarck detested him as the personification of a way of conducting Europe's affairs radically alternative to the one he himself envisaged. The Liberal party he helped to create and led till 1894 became a sociological model for European political commentators, including the Italian Marco Minghetti, the Russian Moisei Ostrogorski and the German Max Weber. To Weber Gladstone represented the 'ideal type' of a new kind of democratic statesman, the Caesaristic–plebiscitary charismatic leader that he examined in *Politics as a Vocation* (1919). In Weber's time the reason for the German failure to generate 'a Gladstonian coalition' became a major question in German political and constitutional historiography and has remained so ever since.

Gladstone has been at the centre of renewed debate and interest since the mid-1980s. On the one hand, he has again become a topic of political discussion, as Thatcherite Conservatives have claimed his heritage as a public financier and political moralist. More recently, he has been elevated as the 'prophet' for a renewed, non-socialist Labour party.[2] This is in line with a long tradition stretching back to Gladstone's own day. As K. O. Morgan has written, '[t]he Liberal Party rallied around Gladstone's "guiding principles" until the 1930s, while Labour pioneers like Hardie, Henderson and Snowden viewed Gladstone as one of their heroes'.[3]

On the other hand, the scholarly literature on Gladstone has grown considerably, both in quantity and in quality. While H. C. G. Matthew, in his magisterial edition of the *Diaries*, has thrown new light on Gladstone's personality and achievements, other historians – from Derek Beales to Boyd Hilton, J. P. Parry and R. T. Shannon – have offered major reassessments of various aspects of his politics. The discussion has also been enriched by the contribution of many North American specialists – including Bruce L. Kinzer, Ann P. Robson, Ann Pottinger Saab and P. T. Marsh – who have proposed a distinctively transatlantic interpretation the full implications of which have yet to be fully appreciated in Britain.

The interpretation offered in the present short book reflects some of the achievements of the above-mentioned scholars, and betrays the extent of the author's debt to H. C. G. Matthew. Thematically – rather than chronologically – structured, this work argues that Gladstone's political activities and convictions can best be understood in the context of the changing relationship between rulers and ruled in nineteenth-century Western Europe and North America. The formation of mass party organizations, the role of the press and the evolution of forms of charismatic leadership will be discussed. Gladstone's understanding of finance and taxation, as well as of international relations and the future of the United Kingdom and British Empire were influenced both by his classical education – then typical of most of the European aristocratic ruling elite – and by his ecumenical Christianity, particularly in his sense of a 'Christian Europe' within which Britain had developed and flourished. These also informed his sensitiveness to the strength of nationalism both abroad and at home, when confronted with the claims of Wales, Scotland and Ireland.

1

THE RISING HOPE

Early Formative Influences

In all our Endeavours let us always act in such a manner as to be able to look up to the director of a most Wise and Benevolent Providence, with grateful heart in the days of Prosperity, and humble submission and resignation in the time of Adversity Comforting ourselves in this, that He will make everything work together for good to them that Love and Fear him.[1]

Thus wrote Thomas Gladstones (the original spelling of the family name) to his son, John, in 1787. They were heartfelt words, and John earnestly reciprocated the sentiments and views which they expressed. For two generations the Gladstones had served in Scotland as kirk elders, then a very important position in the local community, with civil, as well as pastoral, responsibilities. The Gladstones were the personification of Max Weber's 'Calvinistic ethic', fostering 'the spirit of modern capitalism'. Their faith was strong, 'dogmatic, concerned with correctness of belief about God and man, and with the inner isolated life of the individual'.[2] It gave them an extraordinary energy, a tough outlook on life's challenges, and a strong individualism, built around the Calvinist and Evangelical notion of freedom of conscience. The latter apparently accounted for Thomas's approval of George Washington, whom he saw as a sort of latter-day Covenanter engaged in a holy struggle against human arrogance and power.

In 1746 Thomas (1732–1809) reluctantly moved from the Lowland town of Biggar to Leith, the port of Edinburgh on the Firth of Forth, in search of better economic prospects. Once there he managed to build

4

up a solid position as a businessman. His life and outlook were greatly enriched by the woman he married, Nelly Neilson (1739–1806), a merchant's daughter. It was in Leith that their fourth son, John, was born in 1764. The father of the Victorian statesman, John was destined to achieve an even more brilliant business career which would lead him to rise through the ranks of society. By the time he died in 1851, he was a prosperous country gentleman who not only owned two major estates, but also retained an interest in commerce and colonial trade. Yet his beginnings had been fairly humble: after leaving school at the age of thirteen, John became an apprentice in a local ropeyard, and joined his father's corn-chandling business at the age of seventeen.

From his Calvinist forebears John inherited the virtues of self-discipline and self-confidence,[3] as well as a simple Christian faith. From his apprenticeship in the ropery he developed an interest in international trade. By 1787 his ambition had outgrown the limited opportunities of the family Leith-based business, and, like many other Lowland businessmen, he moved to Liverpool to set up a partnership with another Scot, Edgar Corrie.

It was at this stage that, for business convenience, John dropped the final 's' in the family name, which then became Gladstone. Something else which John dropped a few years later was his Presbyterianism. The change did not reflect any major theological or doctrinal evolution on his part, but was due to several reasons of a different, mainly environmental, nature. On the one hand, there was the fact that English Presbyterianism was by then Unitarian. Though John worshipped with the Unitarians for a while, inevitably he found their rationalism and liberal Protestantism distasteful. It was a form of religiosity very different from the orthodox Calvinistic family faith back in Leith. On the other hand, the Liverpool Scots kirk, which John and other immigrants founded in 1792, apparently provided neither the spiritual atmosphere which he desired, nor the connections and contacts which an ambitious, rising businessman like himself would need. As a further milestone on the Gladstones' route into the English establishment, by 1804 John had moved into the Church of England.

The denominational change was helped by John's new family connections. His first wife, Jane Hall, was Anglican. She was a local merchant's daughter who left him a childless widower in 1798. In 1800 he married again, this time to Anne Robertson, the beautiful daughter of the Provost of Dingwall, in the Highlands. Anne belonged to a gentry family above the Gladstones in the Scottish social hierarchy. Like many other Ross-shire aristocrats in the post-Jacobite era, she was an Episcopalian, and when she joined her husband in Liverpool the Church of England may well have offered a suitable answer to her spiritual needs. They were married in the Anglican parish church of St Peter's, yet their eventual decision to move into the Church of England was the outcome of a slow evolution. From a theological point of view it reflected a reasserting of, rather than a weakening of, the Protestantism of the family tradition, as Anne's views were even more intensely Evangelical than those of her husband's.

Meanwhile the family business had prospered: John's personal fortune amounted to £40,000 by 1799. By 1801 he had dissolved the partnership with Corrie, and, with his brother Robert, set up a new business, which lasted until 1821. By 1803 they had acquired a growing interest in the tropical products of Demerara, which the British had recently seized from the Dutch. In the following years the family fortune grew rapidly, with their profits in the West Indies being higher than the ones they derived from other investments. By 1821, when Gladstone established a new partnership with George Grant and John Wilson – thus merging the family's East and West Indies interests in a broader concern – his assets amounted to over £330,000, of which more than half was invested in the West Indies. It was typical of the man that, in contrast to many contemporary Evangelicals, he did not feel that slavery, on which his wealth was increasingly dependent, should cause him any problem of conscience. Though he did not defend slavery in the abstract, he denounced the Evangelical abolitionists as political 'revolutionaries'. Moreover, he argued that the blacks were 'happier' when 'forced to work', that their labour was essential to the prosperity of the colonial economy, and protested that 'it was not for him to seek to destroy a system that an over-ruling of Providence had seen fit to permit in certain climates since the very formation of society'.[4]

With economic success came political ambition and prestigious connections, the most important of which were George Canning and William Huskisson, both in turn MPs for Liverpool and spokesmen for 'liberal Toryism'. John himself entered Parliament in 1818, though not for Liverpool, as he would have wished, but for the borough of Lancaster. He found the 'rottenness' of his constituency too expensive, and in 1820 opted for the cheaper borough of Woodstock, where the influence of the Duke of Marlborough was paramount. As an MP he was not very successful, and his aspiration to sit for Liverpool was continually frustrated. Full achievement of his social ambitions came only in 1846, when Sir Robert Peel nominated him for a baronetcy, a title promptly granted by the Queen.

Thus, William Ewart – so named after his father's most loyal friend – was born into a family which was well established both economically and socially, and on its way up. His early religious education was deeply shaped by the characteristic combination of Scottish fervour and Anglican Evangelicalism. The boy's intellectual environment was dominated by female figures, notably his mother, her friend Hannah More and Anne Mackenzie, William's elder sister. The feeble health and physical frailty of both his mother and his sister inspired reverence in the young William, whose veneration for the latter was further strengthened when she died unmarried and 'sainted' at the age of twenty-six (1829). To their example – if not to their theological views – the statesman always remained faithful.

However, as S. G. Checkland has pointed out in his seminal *The Gladstones. A Family Biography* (1971), these women's spiritual influence was counterbalanced by his father's drive for success and power. The decision to send him to Eton was a typical outcome. Eton and Oxford were perceived by John Gladstone as the passport to that social and political success which he had been unable to achieve: the Gladstone brothers were expected to emulate Robert Peel, himself the son of a calico printer, in the path from business to power. It is important to note that such gentrification did not involve any decline in the family's entrepreneurial spirit: there was simply a division of labour among the brothers. The task of continuing the mercantile tradition devolved upon Robertson, the second son, who received a more practical training at Glasgow College. But Thomas and William were expected to consolidate the family fortune in a different way.

Yet Eton and Oxford involved the risk of spiritual compromise, for, as his parents knew, religious life there had little in common with the rigorous Evangelical spirituality with which their children had grown up, and which played such an important role in their Liverpool life. Thomas, the first Etonian Gladstone, bore the brunt of the experiment, which turned out to be a painful one. The Gladstone children found Eton rather 'pagan', and Tom was particularly frustrated by his inability to live up to his parents' expectation that he would set a good example. There was indeed little scope for nonconformity in Eton life, but Tom's disapproval of his teachers and 'dames' (landladies) was the source of endless trouble for him and much concern for his parents, who feared that he would be expelled. However, far from sympathizing with Tom's plight, John Gladstone was determined that his son should stay at Eton, earn his entrance to the national elite, and master that classical, polite education which he understood to be essential for social success and political advancement.

William enjoyed his schooldays much better than Tom, or indeed than many of his contemporaries, and for the rest of his life preserved fond memories of his time there. Some of his school notebooks have been preserved among the Hawarden papers. Carefully annotated in Gladstone's typically clear handwriting (already recongizable), they contain Etonian exercises in classics and mathematics, decorated with drawings and caricatures (chiefly male profiles and faces), which provide evidence of William's artistic gifts and of his sense of humour.

His Christian faith survived exposure to Eton 'decadence', and in fact he emerged from the trial intensely aware of the need for a revival of the Church. The latter he had learnt to idealize as something which transcended any of its members and ministers, and required absolute loyalty and devotion from individuals as well as government. Both in his political career and in his private life, the chief concerns were his faith, the defence of the Anglican Church and the establishment of Christian values.

According to his mother, Gladstone experienced 'conversion' in 1818–19, but the statesman always preferred to speak of his own spiritual experience as a process which evolved only gradually from the teaching he received from his parents. During his time at Eton and Oxford he continued Evangelical practices, such as the daily study of the Bible, and remained committed to the doctrinal foundations of Anglicanism, particularly the Thirty-nine Articles and the Prayer Book. However, he gradually moved away from most beliefs associated with Evangelicalism and became attracted to the Oxford Movement, which from 1833 was to play a major role in the revival of the High Church. The turning point was probably his acceptance of the doctrine of baptismal regeneration in 1828, accompanied, in the early 1830s, by a growing reverence for the *Book of Common Prayer* and the notion of the corporate church, with its historic line of bishops stretching back to Apostolic times. Gladstone, who had been impressed with the idea of the unity of the Church during his first visit to Rome in 1832, gradually adopted High Church views on a variety of theological matters. In particular, Gladstone abandoned the Calvinist notion that sacraments were mere *symbols* of God's grace and the Lord's Supper the commemoration of Christ's sacrifice. Instead, he came to accept the view that the sacraments were God's *means* of conveying grace, that the Eucharist represented spiritual food 'rather than remembrance', and that the 'apostolic succession' added to the sacrality of the ministry. On each of these points he drew closer to the Tractarians. To the Anglican creed and the principle of its Establishment Gladstone was always to remain faithful, though several adherents of the Tractarian Movement were eventually to move into the Roman Catholic Church. He considered the conversion to Catholicism of some of his friends, including Manning (the future cardinal), and of his sister Helen, as aberrations, which seriously undermined his relationship with both of them. His peculiar stance between High Church and anti-popery was further evidenced when he sponsored the creation of an Anglo-Prussian bishopric of Jerusalem in the early 1840s: Anglo-Catholics such as Newman, who loathed continental Protestantism, were outraged.

Indeed, there were ways in which the family's Calvinist heritage lived on in the young High Anglican politician. In particular, he did not lose the sense of the religious responsibility of the individual, standing alone before his God. This typically Protestant psychological feature is also reflected in William's diaries, which he kept faithfully for over sixty years until failing eyesight and illness forced him to discontinue the practice in 1896. Most of the entries are lists: they include the names of people he met, books he read, and social events he attended. With occasional short, introspective sections, the diaries represent a major exercise in bookkeeping, which Gladstone may have used in his prayers, almost as if he tried to give account to the Almighty for the way he spent his time. Here are two examples, a typically concise one and a more detailed, longer one, from January 1826:

20. Friday.
Friday's business – saw Berthomier. Keate very savage – Read Gray's Long Story &c. – Wrote home to dear Mother – did some holiday task.
21. Saturday.
Finished and showed up holiday task. Part of the Bible from wh it is taken difficult to put into the shackles of verse, on account of its extreme sublimity, &, at the same time, simplicity. Saturdays business. Read papers at Society room. Vice President for the next week. Read gertrude of Wyoming: & read up a little Homer – got things into

order, & prepared to start in the old routine on Monday, please God
– who I trust will be my guide & my defender.[5]

With this vivid sense of spiritual responsibility came an acute awareness of sin. The latter notion provided him with a major explanatory
model which could be applied to interpret the operation of God's
providence in one's life, as well as in the life of the nation. It was
accompanied by the urge to bring others to the truth and salvation.
Ultimately the latter remained a matter of individual awareness, however mediated by the Church through the sacraments, which meant
much more to him than to his Evangelical forebears. A third Calvinistic
feature was his emphasis on discharging one's duty and accepting,
without exultation or moaning, both success and failure, triumph and
defeat. A fourth feature was its work ethic, a drive to succeed reinforced, rather than weakened, by the fact that success was not seen as
an end in itself, but as a means to the fulfilment of the potential and
gifts that God had bestowed on him. This was a component of his
success at first, Eton, and later, at Oxford.

Oxford and Beyond

At Oxford Gladstone excelled in both classics and mathematics and was
awarded a double first in 1831. Classical literature was to remain one of
his lifelong interests, and his command of both Greek and Latin was
extraordinary even by the standards of the time. The three authors
whose thought was to play an important role in Gladstone's intellectual
development were the most 'classical' among the classics: Aristotle,
Plato and Homer.

Aristotle's influence was particularly significant: the ancient philosopher provided young Gladstone with an intellectual foundation on
which the mature Victorian statesman was to build for the rest of his
life. Natural law and a 'communitarian' approach to politics – the
notion that man is a political animal and society and government
are natural institutions – were the central pillars of this framework.
He believed that 'A state of graduated subordination is the natural law
of humanity.... Civil government then is not a matter of option but of
nature.'[6] His leading categories of analysis were the family, the local
community and the state; his vision of a stable society was one in which

everyone knew their place and performed their social and political duty. Aristotle was supplemented by Plato, mainly through the latter's notion of the perfectibility of society – utopian conservatism – which, in the late 1830s, was to become central to Gladstone's view of a Christian kingdom.

Gladstone's Toryism was quintessentially romantic. With its Platonic and Aristotelian convictions, it was in tune with Edmund Burke's and S. T. Coleridge's organicist view of the state. Its emphasis on the latter's collective nature as an organism with a life and character of its own, rooted in the common past, was both illiberal and anti-individualist. In contrast to the contractualism of the Locke tradition and the universalism of the Enlightenment, this romantic approach emphasized historical specificity, the distinctiveness of particular eras and the importance and individuality of national traditions. Gladstone's newly found High Church spirituality was reinforced by these views, and particularly by reverence for tradition, continuity and collective history. Such values contrasted sharply both with the universalism of Protestant teaching, and with the spiritual individualism of the Evangelicals.

It was a well-rounded Tory world-view which found further confirmation in the communitarian sociological model of the Homeric system. In particular the *Iliad* – one of the staples of his Eton studies – provided the ideal of a deeply religious aristocratic society, sustained by values such as chivalry, generosity and friendship. In political terms, Gladstone saw in the world of the *Iliad* a mirror of his youthful romantic Toryism: a constitutional monarchy, limited by the fear of the gods and the deliberations of the assemblies. The latter were the equivalent of a 'parliament': they were led by the noblemen, but within them the popular voice was respectfully considered. If the *Iliad* was so evocative, the *Odyssey* – which reflects a new individualism and sensitivity towards existential choices – may have appealed to Gladstone's residual Calvinist individualism, thus helping to mediate between his Evangelical background and his newly adopted High Church affiliation.

Gladstone's pantheon of intellectual guides was completed by three other authors: the thirteenth-century Italian poet, statesman and political thinker Dante Alighieri; the eighteenth-century divine and philosopher Joseph Butler; and Edmund Burke. Under the influence of Arthur Hallam, his closest friend at Eton, Gladstone developed a real veneration for Dante, whose writings he regarded not solely as a source of enjoyment, but also as a vigorous discipline for the soul. Gladstone felt a strong affinity for the Florentine poet's Christianized

Aristotelianism, for his anti-papal Catholic Christianity – which could be read as a medieval equivalent of Victorian High Anglican views – and for his emphasis on the reciprocal independence (but without separation) of Church and State. This last point Gladstone was to find increasingly attractive as his familiarity with nineteenth-century Italian problems grew from the 1850s onwards.

Dante further strengthened Gladstone's sense of the unity of Europe as a Christian civilization whose international relations ought to be regulated by God's laws. Gladstone also developed his vision from a variety of other sources, notably the Anglo-Catholic notion of the unity of the Church in its different branches (whether Anglican, Catholic, Eastern Orthodox, or the national Protestant confessions). Moreover, Dante's emphasis on the two universal governments (the German-led Holy Roman Empire in the 'temporal' sphere, and the Catholic church in the 'spiritual' one) helped to strengthen Gladstone's idea of the bonds which ought to bind together the Christian nations of Europe.

Finally, on a more personal note, Dante's idealization of his lost love Beatrice in the *Paradiso* struck a deep chord among Victorian romantics, and contributed to the young Gladstone's construction of gender roles. A saintly womanhood – frail and ethereal – was of course resonant with his own experience of family women, particularly his mother and his deceased sister Anne. Intense religiosity and physical disability seemed to be the qualifications required in order to become guardians of human moral and spiritual life.

At Oxford Gladstone was introduced to Bishop Joseph Butler's philosophy, and was particularly impressed by his *Analogy of Religion* (1736). From Butler he derived both an elaborate doctrine of Providence, and a method of inquiry and decision-making. As far as the latter was concerned, Butler recommended careful collection and weighing of evidence as the prerequisite to a resolute course of action. His principle of analogy had widespread application: for there was a correspondence or 'analogy' between natural and revealed religion, which Gladstone traced in particular between the Homeric texts and the Hebrew Old Testament. His assumption was that both stemmed from the same root, one which was given by God to all mankind at the beginning of time. Gladstone revered Homer's spiritual sensitivity, and, following the Church fathers and the Medieval scholastics, represented him as anticipating the Christian doctrines of Providence and an afterlife of reward and retribution for the righteous and evil-doers respectively. At another level, his Homeric work revealed Gladstone's

awareness of what he saw as the perennial and universal value of
'European civilization'.

Analogy could also be traced between natural and human events – a
principle consistent with the Aristotelian view of natural law – as well as
between comparable human events, for instance in national developments. In politics analogy was both the source of probability and the
best guide to political action in a world in which certainty was rarely
attainable. Thus, as Bebbington has written,[7] Butler taught Gladstone
'how to reconcile uncertainty with moral obligation': the method to
follow implied 'first . . . to amass information, then to weigh the prob-
abilities, and finally, once a decision was taken, to pursue the policy
with undeviating commitment'. This precept fitted Gladstone's tem-
perament, and, rather self-consciously, he adopted it throughout his
political career, often to the consternation of colleagues and the bewild-
erment of political opponents.

Gladstone came to know and admire Burke's thought at a very early
stage, in September 1826.[8] He was immediately captivated by the
writings of the great Anglo-Irish political philosopher, who both
inspired and qualified his fervent Toryism.[9] In fact Gladstone continued to meditate on Burke for the rest of his life, even when he began to
play the rather un-Burkian role of idol and prophet of the Radicals. He
turned to Burke especially at crucial times, such as the 1885–86 Irish
Home Rule Crisis. Praise for Burke's insights and inspiration during
the Irish Question appears frequently in his letters and diaries of 1885
and 1886. For example, on 18 December 1885 he wrote: 'Read Burke.
What a magazine of wisdom he is on Ireland & America!' India was
another area in which Burke towered among the political thinkers, as
he had taught 'England the rights of the natives, princes and people,
and her own duties'.[10] The one major topic on which Gladstone, in his
old age, came to reject Burke was – significantly – the French Revolution, which Burke had famously denounced in his *Reflections* (1790).

What made Burke's influence especially profound, however, was not
just his ideas; it was the way in which they were formulated, his method
of historical assessment, and his sensitivity for tradition and the possibility of change through organic growth. From Burke Gladstone
derived a historicist approach to constitutional conservation through
reform, a 'restorative conservatism',[11] which was to inspire his attitude
to both home and Imperial politics. That this notion could be dynamic
and not very conservative was indicated, years later, by his response to
Charles Darwin's discoveries: Gladstone was one of the few orthodox

Christian thinkers who welcomed *On the Origin of Species* (1859), a work which confirmed his conviction that God operated through organic evolution rather than revolution. It was further confirmation of the soundness of the method of analogy.

Finally, from Burke Gladstone derived his typical pragmatism, which was systematic and yet principled: for, as Burke had written, '[c]ircumstances...give in reality to every political principle its distinguishing colour and discriminating effect. The circumstances are what render every civil and political scheme beneficial or noxious to mankind.'[12] At political junctures he valued 'what may be termed appreciation of the general situation and its result'.[13] Accordingly Gladstone became convinced that *'ideals in politics are never realised'*,[14] a view which contrasted with Plato's idealism and notion of perfectibility.

On this basis Gladstone developed his conception of the relationship between Church and State, which he enunciated in two major books – *The State in Its Relations with the Church* (1838), and *Church Principles Considered in Their Results* (1840). These represented the first (and last) consistent expressions of the romantic conservatism which Gladstone had elaborated at Eton and Oxford. *Church Principles* made no major impression on contemporary culture, but was a fair exposition of its author's Anglo-Catholicism and enduring debt to Evangelicalism. By contrast his previous book, *The State in Its Relations with the Church*, was very controversial. In it Gladstone tried to reaffirm the theory of a close link between the Church of England and the English state, one which had somehow been shaken and undermined by the great Nonconformist revivals, the repeal of the Test and Corporation Acts (1828), Catholic Emancipation (1829), and the 1832 Reform Act. Arguing that the state had a conscience and that the distinction between truth and error in matters of religion was of supreme importance, he presented a rather clumsy argument that the maintenance of the establishment of Anglican Christianity was one of the state's primary duties. By the same token Gladstone tried to effect a difficult compromise between his advocacy of the preservation of the institutional privileges of the Church (though they were accompanied by 'erastian' state control on church matters, which Gladstone found distasteful) and the Tractarians' support for full church autonomy. Furthermore, though Gladstone was unable to contemplate the use of force and the imposition of conformity, he struggled to find arguments which would uphold both his organicist vision of the state and toleration and freedom of conscience. As critics pointed out at the time, the theory he espoused was not only reactionary, but also utterly inapplicable to contemporary reality: in a celebrated article in the *Edinburgh Review*, the Whig historian Macaulay dubbed Gladstone 'the rising hope of those stern and unbending Tories', bound, in his opinion, to rebel against Peel's moderate leadership as soon as his services could be dispensed with.

Eventually things went the other way, at least in so far as Gladstone's theocratic ideal was destroyed by his practical experience in the 1841–46 Peel administration, when issues such as ecclesiastical reform in Canada, controversies over religious education in England, and state funding for Roman Catholic education in Ireland brought him to admit the ultimate impracticality of his principles of ecclesiastical policy. By 1843 he commented: 'Of public life, I certainly must say, every year shows me more and more that the idea of Christian politics cannot be realised in the state according to its present condition of existence.'[15]

However unrealistic, *The State in Its Relations with the Church* was not a juvenile aberration, and remained an important landmark in Gladstone's political development: in particular, it threw light on his idea of the state as an 'organic body' with a national conscience, rather than a mere aggregate of individuals. Furthermore – as an abstract ideal, rather than as a policy – it was not reneged on: as late as 1845 Gladstone felt he had to resign from Peel's government when the latter increased the state grant to the Catholic Maynooth College in Ireland, a policy which he had openly condemned in his book. Significantly, he then proceeded to vote *with* Peel *for* the grant. It was typical behaviour, dictated by his honour code, rigidly interpreted, but substantially qualified by his growing historicist pragmatism: thus he resigned from the Cabinet out of consistency with the theoretical views to which, he felt, he had committed himself in 1838; then he voted in support of Peel's proposal out of consistency with the views he had come to adopt on pragmatic grounds and in the light of historical experience.[16]

Catherine

The romantic view of women as saints and angels, developed by Gladstone at home on the model of his invalid mother and his sister Anne, was to undergo important modifications over the years, though it has been argued that he never fundamentally changed his mind.[17] An early encounter with a different model of femininity took place at Oxford. It was there that Gladstone first began to interview prostitutes, who were to become the focus of a life-long charitable exercise. Speculation and rumour as to the nature of his relationship with some of these women have always proliferated, but were, and have remained, unsubstantiated. In an age when political careers could be destroyed by sex scandals,[18] Gladstone managed to devote his efforts to the redemption of a number of these 'fallen women' without his reputation or public image ever being tarnished. After his marriage, his wife joined him in his charitable endeavours, and together they helped to found and fund several 'homes of refuge for fallen women' in the 1850s and 1860s. Moreover, Gladstone was on the Management Committee of the Millbank Penitentiary, to which convicted prostitutes were sent. His efforts continued until the end of his life, though he became more prudent in the late 1880s, fearing that his rescue endeavours might be misconstrued and thus damage the Home Rule campaign.

It was in 1838 that Gladstone first showed an interest in Catherine Glynne, the sister of Sir Stephen, the ninth baronet and one of Gladstone's contemporaries at Oxford. Beautiful, lively and athletic (swimming, horse-riding and archery were her favourite sports), Catherine was intelligent, independent, unconventional and uncomplicated. Born in January 1812, she had been tutored at home with her sister. She was a talented pianist (Franz Liszt had been one of her teachers), and had a wide-ranging education both in modern and classical languages and literature, and in Christian theology.

Healthy and vigorous, a woman more different from Gladstone's female family stereotypes would have been difficult to find. With Gladstone's mother she shared Christian piety (though Catherine's was uncomplicated and never obsessive). An aristocrat with illustrious connections – including Pitt the Younger (her cousin) and Lord Grenville (her uncle), who had led the 1806 cabinet of 'All the Talents' – Catherine was self-confident and serene. She was undeterred by Gladstone's earnestness, which turned out to be quite terrifying to other women. When he proposed to her (in Rome, in the winter of 1839) she took her time to decide. A week earlier she had been presented with an advance copy of *The State in Its Relations with the Church*, which she read with an interest and speed which must have convinced William that she was, indeed, the woman for him. Though the validity of the test was questionable, he was right. To Gladstone's unrestrained delight, Catherine accepted his proposal, though not until June. They were married at

Hawarden on 25 July, in a double ceremony, with Catherine's sister marrying Lord Lyttelton.

The young Gladstone couple could rely on a comfortable lifestyle. Quite apart from Catherine's private means, Gladstone's own share of the West Indian property, which his father had just divided among his four sons, produced a reliable source of income. The fact that his brother Robertson acted as general manager was a further advantage, as William felt free – for a while – from the financial problems and concerns associated with the management of extensive investments.

Though Gladstone has usually been seen or represented as the most Victorian of all Victorians, his married life was in many respects unconventional. It was not just a question of his respecting Catherine's freedom of choice, or the fact that he neither tried nor even wished to subdue her personality to his own. It was a genuine, reciprocally beneficial relationship between two towering personalities. As Marlow has written,

> What Gladstone gave Catherine was a focal point for her unbounding, undirected energies and ambitions, while what she brought into his life was an exhilarating and much needed gust of unorthodoxy. She told her husband, 'What a bore you would have been if you had married somebody as tidy as yourself', but it was not just a question of tidiness. Catherine's bubbling, unpredictable personality saved Gladstone's meticulous sense of order and lack of proportion from crushing or stultifying him.[19]

They took to each other 'like two cherries upon one stalk'. In private, Catherine liberated and inspired his sense of humour and capacity to enjoy himself. In public, she was often by his side encouraging his ambitions, stiffening his resolve and sharing his passions, triumphs and setbacks. On the other hand, William adopted the Glynnes' commitment to the Hawarden estate. Following the 1847 crash of the Oak Farm industrial enterprise in Staffordshire, which his brother-in-law had developed on the credit of his family's estate, Gladstone devoted many years of hard work and massive investment in order to save it from going into liquidation. Hawarden Castle was to become the Gladstones' country home (though they did not own it), where William and Catherine spent intensely happy days whenever he was free from political engagements.

A great social asset because of her family background, Catherine was typically uninhibited and unconventional even in her relationship with the Queen, who liked Mrs Gladstone much better than she did her husband. In contrast to common notions of Victorian sexual prudery, Catherine was not embarrassed by her body, and was in the habit of 'wandering through the castle in a state of *déshabillé* or standing naked by a window calmly having a wash – and Gladstone shared (or learned to share) his wife's physical informality'.[20] Even more extraordinary was the fact that, whenever possible, her husband 'was present throughout Catherine's labours and at the births'.[21] The couple had eight children: William (1840), Agnes (1842), Stephen (1844), Jessy (1845, who died of meningitis in 1850), Mary (1847), Helen (1849), Harry (1852) and Herbert (1854). Though there are no direct references to it in either Gladstone's diaries or his correspondence, it is likely that William and Catherine enjoyed a rather active sexual life.

Yet it was not sufficient for a man of William's energy. His rescue work among prostitutes, already mentioned above, though motivated by a genuine Christian concern, was also a way of letting off steam during political crises and frequent abstention due to distance, pregnancy or menstruation. Gladstone courted temptation, but is unlikely ever to have completely succumbed to it, though his diaries record recurrent emotional stress accompanied by repentance and self-scourging. When in London, Catherine co-operated with William in his potentially embarrassing work among prostitutes, who were regularly invited to their home. While she took much personal care of those whom they 'rescued', her letters to William show few misgivings apart from concern about the danger of physical assault to which he exposed himself while walking in London's East End.

By contrast, Gladstone's relationship with a number of other women, notably the reformed courtesan Laura Thistlewayte, was in a different category from that of 'rescue' work. For over ten years from 1864, when Thistlewayte and Gladstone met, theirs was a very close friendship and, though Laura was 'not Gladstone's mistress in the physical sense', she did fulfil 'the other functions of that office'.[22] His links with Thistlewayte, as well as other female friendships, such as with the dowager Duchess of Sutherland, reflected Gladstone's need for a more intimate intellectual and psychological companionship than Catherine was able to provide.

Later, after the death of the duchess (1868) and the cooling-off of the Thistlewayte friendship, the Gladstone daughters, especially Mary and

Helen, provided an important intellectual support for the ageing statesman. Mary became a protagonist of late Gladstonian Liberalism as one of his private secretaries (1879–86). Helen – one of the first women students at Cambridge, eventually becoming vice-principal of Newnham College – took over from her sister, following the latter's marriage in 1886. For Helen it was a major sacrifice of career to family, but neither Gladstone nor Catherine seemed to realize how much she was giving up for the sake of a Victorian convention. She was able to resume her academic career only after the death of both her parents, and in 1901 became Warden of the Women's University Settlement in Southwark.

The Strange Demise of 'Stern and Unbending Toryism'

Eton and Christ Church completed Gladstone's naturalization as a member of the aristocratic elite. At the same time he became aware of his power as a public speaker, his adroitness in debate, his rousing rhetoric, and his ability to persuade audiences. In 1830–32, with the agitation for the Great Reform Bill under way and passions running high on both sides, William delivered a particularly successful speech at the Oxford Union in defence of Church and State. Encouraged by the response of the audience and comments of his friends, he was soon gratified by the offer of political patronage by the Duke of Newcastle. The offer came through the Duke's son, Lord Lincoln – a friend and contemporary of William's at Oxford – and took the form of the borough of Newark. The latter was still quite 'rotten', despite the 1832 Reform Act, and was regarded as a 'proprietary' borough, where the Duke's influence was paramount for as long as he and his friends were willing to oil the machine. Encouraged by his father, who provided the necessary financial support, Gladstone agreed to stand as a Tory candidate. This decision involved abandoning the great vocation which he had long been considering, the Church. Furthermore, it involved accepting the reality of electoral politics in the days when bribery and free entertainment were the means and price of a Parliamentary career. Like many an idealist politician before and since, the young Oxford graduate professed disgust at the scenes of debauchery and was uneasy about the amount of 'sin' which his electoral agent considered appropriate to foster for the sake of Gladstone's electoral

victory. Fortunately for his sensitive conscience, he was kept blissfully
ignorant of the full extent of his agent's operations.

The decisions to forgo ordination and enter politics instead, with all
the moral compromises which that entailed, have been traditionally
described by historians as the chief examples of John Gladstone's
influence on his son. For William the question involved choosing
between the conflicting wishes of his parents: on the one hand, his
father's voice, urging politics and power; on the other, his mother's,
urging holiness and a life devoted to the defence of the Church and the
true doctrine of Christ.[23] Checkland has argued that such a clash
between power-oriented pragmatism and Christian idealism was to
characterize each phase of Gladstone's life. Usually the outcome of
such conflict was a compromise: thus in the 1830s young Gladstone
'contemplate[d] secular affairs chiefly as a means of being useful in
church affairs'.[24] His justification was that in 1831, at the height of
the Whig and Radical campaign for reform, the Church seemed in
danger of soon being disestablished, and thus in need of able political
advocates. Though this thesis is very suggestive, there are also indica-
tions that the appeal of a political career had been apparent at a much
earlier stage: one surviving piece of evidence is that the Eton schoolboy
wrote 'Right Honourable W. E. Gladstone, M.P.' on a number of envel-
opes, which he then carefully preserved.

Once in the House of Commons Gladstone gradually moved away
from his father's political positions. Yet his early career at Westminster
was informed by filial piety as much as by his own personal conservatism. For instance, what he regarded as his maiden speech, in 1833, was
devoted to the defence of West Indian slavery, an institution which he
condemned in principle but defended against what he saw as a hasty,
irresponsible and demagogically conceived policy of abolition. He
denied allegations of cruelty by the slaveowners (of whom his father
was a leading representative), and defended the considerable investments made by the planters and the rights of property, even though, in
their case, such property was human. As slavery was doomed anyway,
the real issue at the time was that of compensation for the planters, and
the length and type of apprenticeship for the emancipated slaves. The
latter was in fact a temporary substitute for slavery, though in theory
aimed at 'preparing' the former slaves for freedom. Five years later, in
1838, Gladstone spoke again in defence of the slaveowners' interests,
this time against the shortening of the apprenticeship period (which
the Whig Parliament actually terminated in that year). Though in

previous years Gladstone had privately argued that the moral education and personal rights and comforts of the slaves should be more
immediate objectives than their emancipation, the extent to which he
really believed in the policy he defended in 1833–38 is debatable.
However, there is no doubt that he desperately *wanted* to believe in it,
largely out of a sense of filial piety and allegiance to the family's West
Indian interests. His father must have understood that, on this particular issue, William's loyalty rested on thin ice: early in 1838, when
William asked his permission to visit the West Indies in order to find
out for himself about working conditions on the family estate, John
vetoed the trip. Gladstone, who believed in obedience to parents as a
Christian duty, did not go. Yet his opinion of the slavery question was
changing, and continued to change throughout the 1840s: in 1845–46,
as Colonial Secretary, he devoted much of his energy to the termination
of the Spanish and Brazilian slave trade.

After a brief experience in the 1834–35 minority Conservative government, Gladstone's great opportunity came in 1841 with the formation
of the Peel administration, which enjoyed a substantial parliamentary
majority. Resisting Gladstone's demand for the Irish department, Peel
posted him to a rather more technical and less emotional branch of
the government, the Board of Trade, first as vice-president and then
(1843) as president, with a seat on the cabinet.

The Board of Trade provided, as Peel hoped, an effective antidote to
Gladstone's theocratic dreams and archaic Anglican idealism. In fact,
Gladstone soon came to realize the full extent of the United Kingdom's
economic problems. He concluded that the government could do
much to improve trade figures, and, with them, the lot of the common
people and the stability of the state. He felt that it was his mission to do
something about it: indeed, the quasi-religious attitude entailed can
be seen from the fact that '[b]y 1845 time spent on [departmental]
"business" was counted with study and devotion as time spent in a
Godly way'.[25]

Full immersion in the details of administrative reform helped him to
discover his gifts as a public administrator: within a few months he
mastered the intricacies of the British system of trade tariffs (including
the Corn Laws), as well as political economy, which had not been part
of his syllabus at Oxford. Gladstone's religious conception of the state
influenced his attitude to classical economics. Though not totally
immune from the influence of contemporary utilitarianism – in particular, he always remained a supporter of the controversial 1834 Poor

Law system – he was unimpressed by advocacies of dogmatic laissez-faire. As President of the Board of Trade, he was ready both to interfere with and to regulate 'the operations of the market' whenever such a course of action seemed advisable. Indeed, his own 1844 Railway Act – passed at the height of the railway mania – reserved important rights to the state. The companies had to run a low-cost service (with fares not exceeding one penny per mile) each working day of the week; the train was to have covered carriages, stop at every station, and maintain a speed of at least twelve miles per hour. Moreover, the government reserved the right both to interfere with and further to regulate the working of the companies, and to nationalise the lines at twenty-five years' purchase.

A similar combination of religious motivation, empirical assessment of the situation and the influence of the economists also stood behind Gladstone's gradual conversion to the repeal of the Corn Laws. The issue was not only difficult in the technical sense of the word, because of the fall in revenue that a policy of repeal would involve. It was difficult especially in political terms, as repeal could cause the fall of the government and a split in the Conservative party, which had just recovered from a decade of political impotence. The issue had been at the forefront of politics since at least 1815, and the principle of agricultural protection mattered much more than the particular benefits of the laws. The repealers included most of the front bench and the leading lights of the party; but most backbenchers and a large proportion of the Conservative voters, especially those representing the powerful land interest, were protectionists.

As Gladstone became acquainted with the commercial needs of the expanding industrial economy, he looked beyond the question of the Corn Laws and became a supporter of a gradual move towards general free trade. In 1842, as Vice-President of the Board of Trade, he had begun a revision of the tariff system, with a view to relieving trade and industry without upsetting the land interests. There was nothing new in this strategy: in a sense it was the old 'Tory liberal' programme. However, the context was new, with the campaigns of the Anti-Corn Law League in full swing and Chartism agitating a large portion of the artisans and other manual workers. There was a climate of ideological and social confrontation, comparable to the one which had characterized the Reform agitation of 1830–32. One of the instruments whereby Peel and Gladstone were able to stabilize the revenue and release social tension was the income tax, which Peel introduced in 1842 to make up for reductions in indirect taxation. Reforms which did not negatively affect the landed interest were more acceptable than others: thus in 1845 Gladstone repealed the export duty on coal, and removed duties from more than 400 other articles. By contrast, those on imported corn remained intractable: in 1842 Gladstone proposed a reform of the 'sliding scale' of protective duties which included the virtual abolition of protection once the price of wheat had risen above 61 shillings per quarter. Peel found this scheme politically unacceptable, and amended it by increasing the threshold to 73 shillings. It was a reasonable compromise from a political point of view, but many (including Gladstone) feared that it did not go far enough. There was a feeling abroad in Peelite circles that if the revised tariff proved insufficiently flexible to allow the prompt importation of wheat in the case of a bad harvest, the Corn Law system ought to go: that is why the Irish Potato Famine of 1845 was perceived as a final test, despite the fact that Ireland was only marginally affected by the Corn Laws. The Peelites had already made up their minds as to the economic advisability of repeal: the Famine convinced them of its political necessity. By then the party was deeply divided as to what it ought to be conservative about: whether it was the traditional land interest with the Corn Laws, or whether the latter ought to be sacrificed in the cause of the stability of the state and the economy.

Even before the beginning of the Famine Gladstone had begun to show concern about the economic conditions of Ireland. In the autumn of 1845, after resigning office over the Maynooth grant, Gladstone planned 'a working tour in Ireland . . . with the purpose of looking at close quarters at the institutions of religion and education of the country and at the character of the people'.[26] His travelling companions were to be his friends Hope-Scott and Philip Pusey, but the trip had to be called off when Pusey pulled out, and Gladstone had to go urgently to Baden-Baden, where his sister Helen had fallen ill. On his return at the end of the year he was invited to join the Cabinet again as Secretary of State for the Colonies. By then both the Famine and the Corn Law crisis had begun (indeed, Gladstone replaced Stanley, who had resigned over the protection issue).

In retrospect, Gladstone's move towards tariff reform proved an important step towards liberalism. However, at the time, and for years after the party had split, he still regarded himself as a 'free-trade Conservative'. Yet the meaning of this label was becoming increasingly problematic, as personal relations with colleagues and backbenchers were poisoned by a considerable divergence on this most vital matter of public policy. Even his own family was divided on the issue: 'my father is so very keen in his protective opinions, and I am so very decidedly the other way of thinking, that I look forward with some reluctance and regret to what must...place me in marked and public contrast with him'.[27]

He further challenged his father's authority when he joined Disraeli and spoke in support of Russell's Bill to remove Jewish political disabilities, in December 1847. The Bill was occasioned by the election of Lionel de Rothschild as MP for the City of London earlier that year. By then Gladstone had reached the conclusion that a Parliament which admitted Unitarians – 'who refuse the whole of the most vital doctrines of the Gospel' – could not retain any claim to being an Anglican or even a Christian assembly. It was better for Parliament to renounce any pretence of Christianity and return to the Church its rights and independence. Thus, in a way, for Gladstone as well as for his Tractarian friends (who also supported the measure), the emancipation of the Jews tended to foster the cause of the autonomy of the Church in its relations with the state. That Gladstone could contemplate the 'emancipation' of both indicated how far he had moved from the views he had advocated in 1838. It seemed to him that the only alternative to an orthodox Anglican trinitarian assembly was full religious freedom.

But his support for the Jews was motivated by something deeper than simple strategic considerations. In fact it is remarkable that, despite his antagonism to Disraeli, Gladstone retained a life-long sympathy for the Jews as a people. In contrast to the view that they were included in what has been described as his general weariness of 'orientals',[28] there is consistent evidence that he felt a considerable sympathy for the people of the Old Testament. For example, in 1868–74, twenty years after advocating Rothschild's admission to the Commons, he tried (and eventually managed) to persuade the Queen to elevate the Jewish banker to the House of Lords. And in the 1890s, towards the end of his career, Gladstone described the Jews as 'the most oppressed people on earth',[29] and referred to Disraeli's philosemitism as one of the few 'strong liberal convictions' entertained by the Conservative leader.[30] It was as if the Biblical scholar of Evangelical background had once again defeated the party man. It was his mother's voice overwhelming his father's influence.

However, it should be noted that Gladstone was consistently spurred on to embrace liberal causes for motivations which were intrinsically conservative. Thus, despite his evolving opinions on a variety of matters of great political importance, there was not only a certain continuity but also a long-term conservative strategy undergirding his views in both the fiscal and the religious spheres. However, most of his former associates and supporters did not find it very easy to perceive or to appreciate such consistency. The clash of opinion with his own constituents, and especially with his patron, the Duke of Newcastle, had already brought Gladstone to resign his seat at Newark in 1845 and look for another constituency. At the general election of 1847 he stood for the University of Oxford, which returned him triumphantly. However, he was well aware that his constituents had voted for him for a variety of ideologically different – not to say contradictory – reasons: some continued to see in him the old champion of the Church; others had supported the new tariff reformer.

The Colonies and Italy

Of the two roles, the latter soon became the leading feature of Gladstone's public profile. From December 1845 to June 1846 his experience as Colonial Secretary further contributed to opening up his mind to liberal opinions, especially as a consequence of his involvement with the drawing up of new constitutions for Canada and New Zealand. That he became a strong advocate of colonial self-government and the establishment of representative assemblies is hardly surprising, when we bear in mind how much his intellectual framework had been influenced by Edmund Burke, one of the greatest English advocates of the demands of the Thirteen Colonies in the run up to the American War of Independence. However, it was only nine years after the fall of Peel's government that Gladstone offered the fullest expression of his Burkean views in colonial matters. In a speech delivered at Chester, on 12 November 1855, he declared:

> Experience has proved that if you want to strengthen the connection between the colonies and this country – if you want to see British law held in respect and British institutions adopted and beloved in the colonies, never associate with them the hated name of force and coercion exercised by us, at a distance, over their rising fortunes. Govern them upon a principle of freedom. Defend them against

aggression from without. Regulate their foreign relations. These things belong to the colonial connection. But of the duration of that connection let them be the judges, and I predict that if you leave them the freedom of judgement it is hard to say when the day will come when they will wish to separate from the great name of England. Depend upon it, they covet a share in that great name. You will find in that feeling of theirs the greatest security for the connection.... Their natural disposition is to love and revere the name of England, and this reverence is by far the best security you can have for their continuing, not only to be subjects of the crown, not only to render it allegiance, but to render it that allegiance which is the most precious of all – the allegiance which proceeds from the depths of the heart of man.[31]

It must also be remembered that his family's Canningite tradition ensured that Gladstone had always been more 'liberal' in foreign than in home affairs. For example, at Eton he had supported Greek independence, and, echoing Canning, had expressed his disgust for the despotic governments of southern and eastern Europe. Despite the reactionary theories he defended in 1838, by the time the Peel government fell in 1846, Gladstone had discarded most of that 'stern and unbending' Toryism with which he had approached office five years before: he had adopted free trade, relegated his theocratic views to the realm of utopia and developed a new emphasis on representative government.

These were to become central components of the new political position towards which he had begun to move. Appropriately for a man of strong High Anglican convictions, his move towards liberalism did not take the form of a sudden conversion, but of a gradual evolution. His liberal instincts were further strengthened by his opposition to the papacy and the temporal power of the pontiff, and, simultaneously, by his hostility towards Parliamentary attempts to prevent the pope from restoring the Catholic hierarchy in Britain. The latter became a big issue in 1851, when Lord John Russell denounced the pope, on the eve of Guy Fawkes Day, and introduced a Bill to nullify the assumption of territorial titles by Catholic clergy. To the disgust of many former Tories, Gladstone spoke against the Bill, arguing that Parliament '[could not] change the profound and resistless tendencies of the age towards religious liberty'.

Though the initial break with Toryism came over the question of free trade, the final steps had more to do with Italian than with British politics. Like most other upper-class Victorians, Gladstone visited Italy several times (1831, 1838, 1849, 1850–51, 1859 and 1866) and studied its culture and history. The classics provided, of course, a good introduction to Italian studies, but it was Dante and the Italian Romantics who fired Gladstone's emotions and intellect. Dante's thought became an important component of Gladstone's Anglican idea of a non-Roman and anti-papal catholic (i.e universal) Church, whose unbroken heritage stretched across the centuries back into Apostolic times. The Italian Romantics, particularly the Catholic liberals Silvio Pellico and Alessandro Manzoni, whom Gladstone met, typified the continuity of the Dante tradition into modern times. He admired Manzoni's poetry, and translated his ode on Napoleon's death into English, reckoning it to be superior to Byron's work on the same theme. He greatly admired the Christian restraint and resignation which Pellico demonstrated while serving a term in the Moravian fortress of the Spielberg for no other crime than his journalistic advocacy of moderate liberal reforms in Austrian Lombardy. Pellico's book *Le mie prigioni* ('My prisons'), which Gladstone read in 1833, was conceived as a devotional work: yet it had revolutionary effects because it highlighted the contrast between what was perceived as the moderation and the honourable and Christian character of Italian liberals, and the despotic and unreasonable behaviour of the Austrian government. Both Pellico and Manzoni stood for a strongly Christocentric spirituality which could be viewed as closer to Anglican sensibilities than to traditional Catholic religiosity. In the case of Manzoni, this perception was justified by his Jansenistic background and family involvement with Swiss Protestantism.

The political effects of this literary experience were completed by a direct exposure to the repressive machinery of the Neapolitan government, one of the pillars of the Vienna Treaty settlement in Italy. In 1850–51, while enjoying a family holiday in Naples, Gladstone had the opportunity to follow the trial of Carlo Poerio, a minister in the short-lived 1848 Neapolitan liberal government and distinguished intellectual. When the latter was condemned to twenty-five years in the Neapolitan dungeons, Gladstone managed to visit him there and was shocked by the severity of the punishment inflicted on political prisoners. He then realized that he himself had become suspect to the police, who proceeded to censor his correspondence. Thus, the former

Conservative minister was now considered to be a 'dangerous liberal' by Neapolitan standards. Back in Britain, this awareness led him to take action in the form of two *Letters to the Earl of Aberdeen* (April and July 1851), in which he denounced the Neapolitan police state as 'the wholesale persecution of virtue ... the awful profanation of public religion ... the perfect prostitution of the judicial office ... the savage and cowardly system of moral as well as physical torture ... the negation of God erected into a system of Government'.

However reactionary Bourbon rule was, Gladstone's initiative was hardly acceptable to European conservatives, and rather embarrassing for his former associates in Britain. By contrast, he suddenly found himself the hero of the Liberals, both at home and abroad. He was publicly congratulated by Palmerston, then Foreign Secretary, who circulated copies of the pamphlet to British consulates abroad, and Gladstone was regarded for the first time in his career as one of Europe's foremost public moralists – a role which he continued to play till his death, and, posthumously, well into the twentieth century. In a sense, the 'rising hope' had not disappointed, however dismayed 'those stern and unbending Tories' might have been.

2

FREE TRADE AND FINANCIAL REFORM

Public Finance in the 'Age of Atonement', 1846–58

The block on which Peel and Wellington's party had stumbled continued to generate considerable animosity and bitterness among old colleagues long after 1846. As the rump Conservative party under Bentinck, Stanley (Lord Derby from 1852) and Disraeli stuck to the old protectionist cause for a few more years,[1] the Peelites supported Russell's Whig government (1846–52) in a series of free-trade measures, including the repeal of the Navigation Laws (1848–49). In this context it is notable that, although Gladstone's Peelite faith was as strong as ever, he wavered in his support for the government on issues which affected his family's interests, such as, in 1848, the question of compensation for the West Indies sugar planters: this was a difficult pill for the son of the Liverpool merchant prince to swallow, as the planters' profits had already been adversely affected by the application of the free-trade philosophy when the Whigs reduced the tariff preference they had traditionally enjoyed.

Partly for these reasons, after Peel's tragic death in 1850 and the subsequent disintegration of the Peelites as a group, there was an opportunity for Gladstone to return to the party of his youth. However, at the time the Tories had little to offer a brilliant and experienced frontbencher; worse still, for Gladstone the prospect of cooperating with Disraeli, then Conservative leader in the Commons, was not inviting: quite apart from the deepening temperamental and ideological differences between the two men, Gladstone had neither forgotten

29

nor forgiven Disraeli for the latter's vicious attacks on Peel during the 1846 crisis. As Gladstone's secretary recollected,

> He had conceived that Mr. Disraeli was wanting in *character* and in reality of conviction; was 'laughing in his sleeve', and was playing a game of politics as if it were the game of chance; and this want of sincerity engendered a feeling of distrust and apprehension in Mr. Gladstone, as it had previously done in Sir Robert Peel.[2]

Gladstone's relationship with his former party further deteriorated when, after refusing to join the short-lived 1852 administration – headed by Lord Derby and his Chancellor of the Exchequer, Disraeli – he demolished the Tory budget in a celebrated Parliamentary speech delivered on 2 December 1852.[3] Though a defeat of the Derby government was likely even before Gladstone rose to speak, his violent denunciation of Disraeli's financial policy – spectacularly underscored by a violent thunderstorm which raged as the debate progressed – turned the Conservative debacle into a humiliation. Such passion and fire constituted an early display of a feature of Gladstone's personality, one which was to become increasingly prominent as time went on. Years later, Lord Stanley, the future fifteenth Earl of Derby, effectively described it from an anti-Gladstonian point of view:

> Gladstone's own temper is visible and audible whenever he rises to speak...the mixture of anger and contempt in his voice is almost painful to witness. With all his splendid talent, and his great position, few men suffer more from the constitutional infirmity of an irritable nature...Disraeli is quite aware of the advantage which he possesses in his natural calmness: and takes every opportunity to make the contrast noticeable.[4]

Though perhaps hardly compatible with Gladstone's Christian convictions – especially when deployed in the service of his unrelenting hatred for Disraeli – this vehemence may have been more of an asset than Lord Stanley thought. In his recent psychological study, applying 'stress and coping theory', Travis Crosby has argued that 'anger can be an appropriate instrumental device for securing certain psychological ends'. As such it is rationally 'chosen' as 'a strategy to unnerve or intimidate opponents or to unmask opposition policies...to fend off threatening events or behaviour'.[5] The debate on the 1852 budget is a typical example: Gladstone's rhetorical fireworks were no sign of loss of emotional control. Rather, they 'interpreted' Disraeli's budget for the wide audience of his opponents, 'unmasking' his policies, and helped to set the stage for the presentation of Gladstone's own ideas.

The political consequences of this incident were significant. Not surprisingly, the mutual antagonism of Gladstone and Disraeli hardened considerably. There is little doubt that between the two politicians there already were substantial differences. Yet, in order to account for the bitterness of Gladstone's attack we should also bear in mind that, in terms of career prospects, his position was similar to that of Disraeli. They were both bound to see each other as competitors for the same top jobs, especially for as long as the two men were rivals for the leadership of the Conservative party.

The government's resignation was followed by the formation of a Whig–Peelite coalition government under the Earl of Aberdeen, with Gladstone as Chancellor of the Exchequer. The balance of forces within the cabinet reflected both the political weakness of Lord John Russell, and the prestige and influence of the Peelites. The latter, in Parliamentary terms, consisted of a dwindling group of MPs and peers; however, in the new administration they accounted for the Premier and the ·Chancellor of the Exchequer, together with nearly half the members of the cabinet. Gladstone now had the opportunity to become the architect of the British system of free-trade finance. Typically, he did not miss the chance.

He found himself in a much easier position than Disraeli had in December 1852. Then the latter had to devise a system which would provide some compensation to the shipping, sugar and land interests for what they had lost with the repeal of protective duties, and, simultaneously, reassure the country as to the Tories' acceptance of free trade. He had tried to square the circle by reforming and rationalizing the income tax, which in his view would become a permanent feature of the British tax system and would be extended to the lower middle classes. However, his budget – introduced in a provocative speech – was not well received by the House. Gladstone found it 'disgusting and repulsive'. He was angered by Disraeli's rather spurious surplus, and denounced it as a major sin against Peelite orthodoxy. He was even more incensed by Disraeli's proposal to lower the income-tax exemption threshold to £50, a figure which meant that payment would also fall to the lower middle classes, for the benefit, Gladstone argued, of the very wealthy. In contrast, Gladstone's policy was to give every encouragement to trade and personal expenditure, and render the fiscal burden on 'the small people and the working classes' less grievous, thus encouraging upward social mobility. Furthermore, while Disraeli wanted to turn the income tax into a permanent feature of the British fiscal system, Gladstone saw it as a dangerous incentive to government financial irresponsibility and a warlike foreign policy. In fact, he thought that it should be retained only as a temporary device for the purpose of completing the repeal of protective duties and the implementation of free trade. The latter involved the repeal or substantial reduction of duties affecting international commerce and internal consumption.

Introduced in a speech regarded as one of his most brilliant parliamentary performances, Gladstone's 1853 budget was an interesting combination of Peelite financial orthodoxy and a moralist–populist appeal to public opinion as a direct source of political legitimacy. Gladstone proposed 'once more [to] associate the income tax with a remission of duties'.[6] The tax was to be retained (indeed, its operation was to be extended to Ireland), but only as a 'temporary' device for seven years.[7] He planned to repeal it by stages up until 5 April 1860. Apart from lowering the exemption limit from £150 to £100, the income tax, 'this colossal engine of finance', was left 'unreconstructed': Gladstone rejected Disraeli's distinction between 'realized' and 'precarious' incomes as financially unsound. Thus the tax retained its targeting of middle-class incomes, a feature which Gladstone appreciated as an inducement to retrenchment and a deterrent against jingoism: he hoped that, knowing that any increase in military expenditure would immediately affect the rate in the pound, middle-class electors would be more appreciative of the benefits of peace and more aware of the retribution of war.

The income tax and a more comprehensive succession duty (instead of the old legacy duty, which affected personal property only) were presented as twin pillars of a financial system through which social stability and economic growth would be achieved – aims which the propertied classes could see as more than compensating for the nuisance and expense of a moderate contribution to the Exchequer. To the artisans and consumers in general Gladstone offered a systematic reduction or abolition of indirect taxes. Thus, 123 articles were freed from taxation, while customs duties were reduced on 133 others. Besides encouraging consumption at home, the operation was convincingly presented as leading to a steady increase in British exports. In addition, a conversion scheme was introduced, in order to reduce the cost of the servicing of the national debt.

Technically, Gladstone's financial approach was a further development of his Peelite creed: its ingredients were a balanced budget, regular surpluses and a careful consideration of the social and political implications of the various taxes. Taxation should be simple, understandable and easy to collect, and the fiscal burden distributed among the social classes with some degree of equity. The Chartists had clamoured against 'taxation without representation': now Gladstone answered by repealing hundreds of indirect taxes and by lowering the income-tax exemption rate to £100. Thus the income tax corresponded, within certain limits, to the dividing line between those who had the franchise under the 1832 Act, and those who did not. The Chartists had claimed that there should be 'no taxation without representation': now Gladstone had repealed most of the taxes on those who did not possess the franchise. It was the ultimate Peelite response to moribund Chartism. In H. C. G. Matthew's words, this was the substance of the 'social contract' of mid-Victorian Britain:

> The wage-earners were, uniquely in Europe, virtually represented in Parliament by a self-taxing class of income-tax paying electors. Income tax thus reminded the propertied class not merely of its fiscal, but of its political responsibilities; it united also the two factors which Victorians regarded as cardinal to stability in the State: fiscal and political probity.[8]

In fact, such a 'social contract' survived – in its original form – only until 1867, when the electorate was significantly enlarged to include a considerable number of men who did not pay the income tax. But Gladstone's work as the 'liberator' of British trade survived his elaborate plan to relate taxation and the electoral franchise and (with the income tax as a permanent feature) remained the cornerstone of British fiscal policy for generations, even under subsequent Conservative and Labour governments.

This vision reflected not only Gladstone's understanding of political economy and the requirements of the historical situation in which he operated, but also his religious convictions. If his conversion to free trade had been an intellectual change guided by empirical observation and theoretical reflection, the unbending zeal with which Gladstone pursued the establishment of a free-trade system was – literally – religious. It was grounded in Christian ethics and in his typically Protestant sense of accountability to God, and sustained by Gladstone's will to 'make atonement' – in Boyd Hilton's words – for the suffering of the poor. He regarded his fiscal policies 'as being the political and administrative expression of a comprehensive set of moral beliefs'.[9]

On the whole, the 1853 budget was a successful *political* operation, which gave Gladstone's career the boost it needed. Like Disraeli, Gladstone was in a comparatively weak and vulnerable position. In contrast to most other leaders, including Derby and Russell, he did not enjoy the benefits of family connections, influence and patronage – then the mainstays of political power. Moreover, as a Peelite in a coalition government, he did not really have a party on which to rely for support in the House. Faced with such odds, Gladstone elaborated a strategy for turning his weakness into strength. The fundamentals of such strategy were his rhetorical powers and newly developed links with the press. The aims were to reap the political benefits of his well-advertised financial prowess, and to present his own comparative political isolation as a noble stance adopted in the national interest, to which he appealed above the old cliques. From 1853 his style consisted of 'big budgets' – political budgets – presented in long and elaborate speeches with a variety of dramatic effects, which turned even the exposition of dry economic figures into an absorbing representation of a principled struggle for righteousness. He was sustained by rhetorical powers quite extraordinary by any standard:

> His physical and mental force was such that he could speak for more than four hours at a stretch, and with vigour and freshness so sustained that George Venables, an extremely fastidious and not overfriendly critic, after hearing him for four hours, and on a financial subject, wished that he could go on for four hours more.[10]

This strategy also worked because Gladstone, like Palmerston, understood how public opinion operated and how it could be 'worked' through the press. The latter, duly briefed, responded with enthusiasm: *The Times*, The *Daily Telegraph*, the provincial liberal press and, later, the working-class weeklies – all strangely united in the free-trade crusade – celebrated his budgets as patriotic responses to the needs of the economy and the expectations of the people. This appeal to 'the people' was Gladstone's most striking innovation in Peel's financial policies. It was the cornerstone of what H. C. G. Matthew has described as the 'politicization of the Chancellorship'.

The Crimean War

After the 1853 budget there still remained as many as 466 articles of consumption which were taxed: Gladstone had already targeted them for repeal or 'simplification', but the Crimean War forced him to change his schedule and short-term plans. It was in November 1853 that hostilities began between Russia and the Ottoman Empire, following the Czar's attempt to impose, virtually, a protectorate on the Sultan's Christian subjects. Britain and France felt that their interests in the eastern Mediterranean were at stake, while the British government was also nervous about communications with India, in case the Russians captured the Dardanelles and the Ottoman Empire collapsed. Thus, at the end of 1853 the Royal Navy sailed into the Black Sea, following the destruction of the Turkish fleet by the Russians at Sinope. Then, in March 1854, Britain and France declared war on Russia.

Gladstone's attitude to this war was complex. On the one hand, he believed it to be morally justified, because Russia had unilaterally applied force against Turkey in breach of 'international law', or the diplomatic conventions of the 'Concert of Europe'. From this point of view he thought that Britain and France had the right, if not duty, to intervene. On the other hand, deeply sceptical about the Ottoman Empire, Gladstone did not share contemporary British enthusiasm for the war. Indeed, from as early as October 1853, swimming against the rising tide of jingoism and Russophobia, he warned that the consequences of a major conflict would be dire:

> When we speak of general war we do not mean real progress on the road of freedom, the real moral and social advancement of man, achieved by force. This may be the intention, but how rarely is it the result, of general war! We mean this – that the face of nature is stained with human gore; we mean that bread is taken out of the mouth of the people; we mean that taxation is increased and industry diminished; we know that it means that burdens unreasonable and untold are entailed on posterity; we know that it means

that demoralisation is let loose, that families are broken up, that lusts become unbridled in every country to which that war is extended.[11]

Once hostilities began, it became his duty, as Chancellor of the Exchequer, to find the money necessary to fight the war to a successful conclusion. At first he was determined to raise no loans but make the country pay in cash. As he said at the time, he thought that '[t]he expenses of war are the moral check which it has pleased the Almighty to impose upon the ambition and the lust of conquest that are so inherent in so many nations': hopefully the taxman would bring the jingo back to his senses. Accordingly, the income tax was doubled as soon as hostilities began. However, Gladstone's financial rectitude did not survive the first year of military disasters: soon Britain's determination to win resulted in a fresh recourse to both the National Debt and indirect taxation. Before too long Gladstone feared that the length of the hostilities might bring about even a return to protection.

In the new climate it was not just Gladstone's fiscal 'virtue' and financial pacifism which were out of step with the national sentiment, but the whole approach to government personified by its Prime Minister, the pious Lord Aberdeen. Yet important administrative reforms of a Peelite nature could still be steamrollered through Parliament, and were even helped by the climate of national emergency created by the disappointing performance of the British military and administrative machines in the Crimea. In particular, Gladstone was active in pushing through the reform of the civil service, with a view to opening it up to competition and merit through public examinations. The reform followed the publication of the famous Trevelyan–Northcote Report, and reflected the national revulsion against the traditional aristocratic system of patronage, which the war had tested and found wanting. Though hardly revolutionary (the competition system had already been adopted by most European countries and by the East India Company), its adoption by the civil service was vocally resisted even in Liberal circles, and denounced by Russell as 'harshly republican'. Eventually a compromise solution was found, but the civil service did not become fully open to competition until 1870.

While the war was a misfortune for the Peelites, it provided Palmerston with a great opportunity. He had become the most vocal proponent of a vigorous approach to the Eastern Question after resigning from the Aberdeen coalition at the time of the Turkish defeat at Sinope.

Soon back in office, he became the idol of a nationalist public opinion. His star rose increasingly higher from January 1855, when Lord John Russell left the government, which was subsequently defeated and resigned. After a long crisis, Palmerston was asked to form a government, which included Gladstone and a few other Peelites. However, when the Prime Minister decided to accept J. A. Roebuck's motion of an inquiry into the previous government's handling of the Crimean War, Gladstone resigned: he could not be party to a public critique of Lord Aberdeen's policies, of which he had been one of the chief proponents. He had been in office under Palmerston for only a fortnight.

By resigning he attracted to himself an immense amount of criticism: his decision seemed unpatriotic, and was totally out of tune with the nationalistic fervour of the time. As the press and mobs joined in condemning his stance, for a while he had the impression of being the most unpopular man in Britain. There then followed four difficult years in the political wilderness, during which he moved increasingly closer to the Manchester School Radicals, mainly on account of the affinity between their views and his position on matters of finance, administrative reform and foreign affairs. In each of these areas he took a consistently Peelite line, desiring a return to strict retrenchment, further rationalization of the bureaucracy and a compromise settlement with Russia once the Czar had offered peace in the spring of 1855. Gladstone argued that the public law of Europe had been vindicated and Russian aggression had been checked: to him it seemed wrong to continue the campaign in order to force the surrender of the main Russian fortress in the Crimea, Sevastopol. In the jingoistic atmosphere of the time, his position was perceived as mean and perfidious. However, it contained most of the ingredients of his later liberalism.

Despite his alienation from Palmerston, in 1856, when Derby tried to lure him back into the Conservative fold, Gladstone felt unable to accept. Nevertheless in 1857 he cooperated with Derby (and with Cobden) in a joint attack on Palmerston's Chinese policy, in the days of the second 'opium war'. In a political quandary, in 1858 he accepted the position of Lord High Commissioner Extraordinary in the Ionian Islands, which were then seeking unification with the kingdom of Greece: it was a sort of 'classical indulgence', a stylish holiday which allowed him to retain some link with the Conservatives – then in office – without being formally associated with Derby's government.

Though he was personally closer to Derby than to Palmerston, his views were by now recognizably Liberal on certain important issues. These included colonial self-government, freedom of religion, and Italy. The latter was the really hot question in 1858–59, as France and Piedmont were about to begin a war to expel Austria from the Po valley. Always an Italophile and sympathizer with Italian liberalism, Gladstone had become a prominent advocate of the peninsula's independence, apparently after being converted by the Venetian exile Daniele Manin. His zeal was further strengthened in February 1859, when he met the Piedmontese Prime Minister, the Count of Cavour, in Turin.

It was in 1859 that Gladstone finally joined the Liberal camp. The famous meeting at Willis's Room, on 6 June 1859, is generally considered to be the 'founding convention' of the modern Liberal party. It marked the reconciliation between Russell and Palmerston, and laid the foundation for a Whig–Peelite–Liberal–Radical coalition backed by a large Parliamentary majority. In this context Gladstone accepted the position of Chancellor of the Exchequer under Palmerston. Quite apart from the Italian Question, his final decision was influenced by three factors, which had steadily become crucial to his political vision as it had developed since 1846: namely, his free-trade enthusiasm, his zeal for administrative reform, and his detestation of Disraeli.

The People's William, 1859–1867

Back in 11 Downing Street once again, Gladstone was eager to resume both his rationalization of the fiscal system and the extension of free trade. One of the resultant measures for which he became responsible was the 1860 French Treaty, which liberalized trade with Britain's most powerful neighbour. On this occasion he had to defend his policy not only against the protectionist Right, but also against the intransigent free-trade Left, who saw the Treaty as a violation of the principle of the unconditional repeal of tariffs. Relying on Cobden's support, Gladstone argued that no breach of free-trade principles had occurred, as the privileges that Britain accorded to France were extended to all the other nations too.[12] Whatever the orthodox view, the actual outcome of the Treaty was a major boost to the practice of free trade throughout continental Europe, which for the following nineteen years became entangled in a web of treaties for the reduction of import tariffs and trade barriers.

The French Treaty was especially important from a political point of view. In 1859–60 Britain was becoming paranoid about Napoleon III's alleged expansionist designs; fear of a French invasion generated demands for expensive programmes of rearmament. In this context Gladstone used free-trade diplomacy to create a new and more relaxed climate. With the help of Cobden and his French counterpart, Michel Chevalier, he outmanoeuvred the 'hawks' in a successful bid to divert public attention from coastal fortification and battleships to French claret and Parisian gloves. His ploy succeeded and was a step forward in his strategy of 'politicization of the Exchequer': while previously Gladstone had used the budgets to shape a new social balance at home, from 1860 he tried to influence the Foreign Office and restrain the defence departments. He had not forgotten the lesson of the Crimean War – namely, that 'sound economy' at home could hardly be sustained without peace in Europe.

However, it was the national economy – rather than foreign affairs – which continued to occupy most of his time and energy. When Gladstone resumed office in 1859 there were still as many as 419 articles subjected to duty. Within two years their number fell to only 34, including spirits, sugar, tobacco, tea, wine, coffee, corn, currants, timber, chicory, figs and fig-cakes, hops, pepper, raisins and rice. Duties on sugar, tea and coffee were considerably reduced, thus stimulating an increase in popular consumption, which, in turn, generated an enormous boost to the revenue.

The labouring poor were thankful for both prosperity and cheap food, as was demonstrated by the triumphal welcome that greeted Gladstone from the workers during his 1862 visit to Northumberland. His popularity reached a new peak after the repeal of the paper duty, which he had managed to push through Parliament in 1860–61. The paper duty had long been hated by both Chartists and Radicals as a piece of 'class legislation' and check on popular literacy. The political impact of its repeal was increased by the fact that it involved a confrontation between the Chancellor and the House of Lords: eventually Gladstone included the proposed reform in his 1861 budget, which the Lords did not dare to challenge, as they knew that an attack on the annual money bill would create constitutional complications which they would be wise to avoid.

In radical circles the paper duty repeal was welcomed as the abolition of the last vestige of 'taxation upon knowledge', and a vindication of the 'ancient constitution', because the will of the representatives of the 'Saxon' common people had been imposed on the recalcitrant 'Norman' Upper House. Thanks to the obstinacy of the Lords, the repeal – potentially a simple administrative reform – generated a major political incident, confirmed the impression that Gladstone was genuinely concerned about the people, and gained him the nickname of the 'People's William'. From then on his personal popularity among working-class radicals increased by leaps and bounds.

Part of this success depended on his ability to express the essential principles in ways which were readily and universally understandable. His businesslike mottoes of 'small profits and quick returns' and of leaving 'the money to fructify in the pockets of the people' seemed to contain the secret of a flourishing Treasury coupled with the diminution of taxes. His stress on the need for balanced budgets was in tune with popular views of financial morality as consisting in 'making expenses fall within the limits of a fixed income'; moreover, as an assimilation of national finance to that of a well-managed family, it seemed both rational and verifiable. The classical principles of taxation which the 'People's Chancellor' applied were also deeply rooted in popular expectations through readings and popularizations of Adam Smith.

Though Gladstone was revered as the liberator of the 'people's breakfast table', that is, the minister who had removed duties and taxes from many items of mass consumption and necessities of life, he was by no means committed to the repeal of all indirect taxes. As he pointed out,

I am...as between direct and indirect taxation, perfectly impartial....there cannot be a grosser delusion than the supposition that the work of Parliament...has been to destroy indirect taxation. The hand with which Parliament has wrought has been a pruning hand; its thought all along has been not to destroy the tree, but to strengthen the stock; the aim of the operation has been to augment both size and vigour; and the consequence is that at this moment, when indirect taxation has been destroyed, as the fashionable phrase is,...indirect taxation is larger and more productive...than at any former period of our history.[13]

In choosing which taxes and duties to abolish or reduce, Gladstone followed criteria more complex than that of merely encouraging consumption. He maintained that it would be 'a mistake to suppose that the best mode of giving benefit to the labouring classes is simply to operate on the Articles consumed by them. If you want to do the *maximum* of good, you should rather operate on the articles which give them the *maximum* of employment.'[14] He argued that the main advantage of the repeal of the Corn Laws had been not so much the reduction in the price of bread as 'the growth of a regular and steady trade in corn': '[b]y that trade you have created a corresponding demand for the commodities of which they are the producers...and it is the enhanced price their labour thus brings, even more than the cheapened price of the commodities, that forms the main benefit they receive'.[15] Likewise, part of the argument behind the repeal of the paper duty in 1861 was that untaxed paper would boost production and employment, as paper products were used in many different industries, ranging from optical instruments to the manufacture of water pipes, hats and teapots. He concluded that 'by putting in motion an immense trade we shall...give a greater and wider stimulus to the demand for the labour of the country'.[16] At the time, and for many decades afterwards, this constituted the only employment policy, whether devised by financial ministers or demanded by the labour movement.

It should be noted that this strategy did not always work quite as smoothly as Gladstone and other advocates of free trade would have hoped. Some manufactures – such as silk in Coventry after the 1860 French Treaty[17] – suffered severely under unrestricted foreign competition, and declined, generating unemployment in particular trades and areas. On the other hand, such localised unemployment was compensated by the jobs which free trade helped to create in the staple industries throughout the boom years 1850–73.[18] Doubts as to the desirability of unilateral and unconditional repeal of import duties were occasionally voiced during negative trade cycles: this happened especially in 1866, 1869 and 1870, when the number of those in receipt of poor relief was higher than in any year since 1849. Certainly in the early 1870s – at the end of the boom – there was abroad among the working classes an as yet unarticulated discontent. Ultimately, this was to express itself as aspiration to greater security and to release from the straitjacket of a market economy. Free trade had achieved many improvements; yet, more than twenty years after the repeal of the

Corn Laws, poverty and pauperism were far from disappearing, and the economy was still undergoing periodical slumps. Such problems had technical aspects, linked to the as yet very limited knowledge of the workings of an industrial economy in a world still undergoing industrialization: there was no credible strategy for avoiding the cyclical recurrence of slumps. The only known palliatives were those offered by friendly societies and collective self-help, and by trade-union organization.

It is remarkable that, while Gladstone's popularity among the working classes increased, he met with growing resistance among the 'educated' members of society. The latter seemed to have become unresponsive to his calls for further retrenchment, as shown by their support for both the Crimean War and for Palmerston's bellicose foreign policy in 1858–63. It was in this context that Gladstone began to consider the possibility of a further instalment of Parliamentary reform. Frustrated by what he saw as self-seeking aristocratic colleagues in government, baffled by the voters' apparent indifference to further financial reform, Gladstone began to think that the route to greater public economy entailed a revision of the 1832 electoral dispensation and the enfranchisement of the 'moral and responsible' working man – Nonconformist and free-trader to a man.

3

PRIME MINISTER

From Financial Reform to Franchise Reform, 1864–1867

When Gladstone first began to consider electoral reform, around 1864, it was against the background of a series of political disappointments. His drive for ever stricter public economy had repeatedly been boycotted by jingoistic middle-class electors, who supported Palmerston's 'spirited' and (Gladstone thought) expensive foreign policy, instead of following the narrow path of peace, retrenchment and financial virtue. Electoral reform, with the admission of new puritan blood 'within the pale of the constitution', began to appear to him to be the best means to greater financial probity. As we saw in the previous chapter, in Gladstone's view financial reform and the franchise were interdependent: in the 1860s he began to consider whether the former's limits could be enlarged by extending the latter. Thus to Gladstone franchise reform was not a matter of 'democracy', but rather of finding a state of equilibrium between public morality and fiscal probity. He hoped that, once the influence of the middle class on the electoral system had been counterbalanced by Nonconformist artisan puritanism – and related retrenching instincts – it would become easier for the Chancellor of the Exchequer to impose a 'fiscal constitution' on the government's defence and foreign affairs departments.

Therefore, to Gladstone the crucial component of any franchise reform plan was the 'moral fitness' of the prospective electors. His gradual conversion to electoral reform was qualified by his emphasis on 'capacity'. Though at first defined in terms of ability to pay the rates, for Gladstone 'capacity' was always a moral and civic category. He thought that working men had provided evidence of such 'capacity'

43

during the Lancashire Cotton Famine, when they refused to countenance military action against the Union blockade of the cotton ports
of the Confederate States, on the grounds that it would jeopardize the
cause of the emancipation of the slaves and of American democracy.
Though some historians have cast doubt on the validity of Gladstone's
interpretation of working-class attitudes to the Civil War, there can be
little doubt that there was considerable popular support for the North,
especially after President Lincoln's 1863 Emancipation Proclamation.
Furthermore, it must be borne in mind that, contrary to Checkland's
stereotype (see below, p. 58), Gladstone had first-hand knowledge of
working-class attitudes to the American Civil War, since in 1862 he and
his wife had been personally involved in relief activities: for a while they
had provided meals and jobs for about a thousand unemployed Lancashire workers on the Hawarden estate.

It was in this context in May 1864 – in a famous speech which
infuriated the then prime minister, Lord Palmerston – that Gladstone
argued that 'every man who is not presumably incapacitated by some
consideration of personal unfitness or political danger is morally
entitled to come within the pale of the Constitution'. Though he
devoted the rest of the speech to qualifying this bold statement, the
latter was construed by the popular press to mean that Gladstone had
converted to manhood suffrage. It was a misunderstanding: nevertheless it helped to improve the Chancellor of the Exchequer's political
standing among the urban artisans. Moreover, however qualified, the
phrase was indicative of his deep difference from Palmerston, who saw
liberalism as rule of law under a Burkean 'virtual' representation. By
contrast, Gladstone's position was becoming closer to the Aristotelian
model of participatory citizenship for 'the best men', with a typical
emphasis on 'virtue'. By 1865 the latter was ascribed to improving
artisans with deposits in the Post Office savings banks. They deserved
the vote because they had the 'capacity' for it, as was showed by their
'self-command, self-control, respect for order, patience under suffering, confidence in the law, [and] regard for superiors'.[1]

In advocating reform, Gladstone's point was that only those working
men who were prepared to put public interest and moral duty before
class or sectional advantages, demonstrated that they were endowed
with the moral requisite for discharging political duties and enjoying
the related privileges. Gladstone was only prepared to countenance a
limited enfranchisement of some urban artisans, so that they could
represent about thirty per cent of the electorate in some borough

constituencies. Besides his concern for financial reform, in supporting the enfranchisement of a large proportion of the urban working men, Gladstone's aim was to undermine the sense of 'class' exclusion so often lamented by artisan spokesmen since the days of Chartism. Yet he rejected the notion that workers should be encouraged to think of themselves as a 'class' with collective grievances, rather than as individuals with deserved 'privileges'. In legislative terms this attitude translated into a proposed reduction from £10 to £7 of the borough franchise established by the 1832 Act, eventually accepting a further reduction to £5. Even if there seemed to be little popular interest in electoral reform, in Peelite fashion Gladstone saw a moderate extension of the franchise as a pre-emptive strike against a rekindling of popular agitation.

The opportunity to experiment with these plans came in 1865, with the sudden death of Palmerston. The latter had been the chief obstacle to Reform. The new Prime Minister, Lord Russell, and his Chancellor, Gladstone, then began to hammer out a Bill which reflected the above ideas. It was fitting that, as Gladstone approached Parliamentary reform and a bolder kind of Liberalism, he was forced to leave his Oxford constituency for a more popular seat in Lancashire.

The Liberal Bill was far too moderate to awaken the interest of public opinion, but, surprisingly, it gave rise to a strong opposition in the Commons, particularly among dissident Liberals. One of them, Robert Lowe, managed to offend both the popular press and the working-class political organizations by arguing publicly that the 200,000 new voters which the Bill proposed to register were a depraved and corrupt mob, unworthy of political rights. His words, underscored by the House's determination to reject the government's Bill, evoked a strong reaction among the artisan reform associations and – for the first time – the new trade unions. These organizations had contemptuously shunned the Reform Bill when it was first proposed by Russell and Gladstone: now that it had been rejected they suddenly adopted it. The collective identity of the Victorian urban artisan hinged on values such as 'self-respect', 'independence' and patriotism, qualities which were more common and deeply rooted than any ideology of democratic rights. By questioning these values, Lowe and the other anti-Reformers had unwittingly played into Gladstone's hands.

The 1866–67 reform agitation provided one of the first illustrations of the national dimension of the popular Liberalism which had emerged from twenty years of free trade, administrative reforms and economic progress. This Liberalism was based on a mass emotional response to a moral challenge; in it 'passion', rather than rational calculation, played a considerable role. Though at times difficult to control, 'passion' provided Liberalism with genuine mass support, and helped to involve not only the radicals, but also innumerable common people without a developed political conscience. In 1866, as on successive occasions, Gladstone displayed a remarkable sensitivity towards the moods and susceptibilities of the masses. It was a question of style as much as of content.

The Liberal government was voted down following the defection of Robert Lowe's faction of anti-reform Liberals (the Adullamites),[2] and resigned. In a way this called the bluff of the anti-Reformers and made them face the consequences of their political miscalculation. A minority Conservative government, led first by Lord Derby and then by Benjamin Disraeli, felt bound to propose an alternative Reform Bill. Moderate in its original form, it was soon taken over by the Parliamentary Left, as the government lost control of the debate. Eventually it was passed in July 1867 – against the advice of most Tory backbenchers and with a series of important amendments introduced by the Radicals. The outcome of this unusual procedure was a far more democratic measure than most politicians, including Gladstone, would have found acceptable in 1866. The circumstances forced both party leaders to take what they saw as a 'leap in the dark' of limited democracy. Despite Maurice Cowling's influential analysis, there is little doubt that mass demonstrations – including the famous Hyde Park riot in 1867 – and 'pressure from without' by organizations such as the Reform Union and the Reform League affected Gladstone's outlook, as well as the Parliamentary debates.

The most important changes introduced by the Second Reform Act affected the boroughs, where the vote was conferred on all male ratepayers, irrespective of property qualifications, but subject to a twelve-month residence qualification. This resulted in a dramatic change of their electorate both in terms of numbers (which were doubled), and social composition (manual workers became the single largest group in many boroughs).

The 1867 Reform Act had not been of Gladstone's doing, and historians have sometimes suggested that Disraeli benefited from the new franchise dispensation, an interpretation which would seem to be corroborated by the Conservative victory of 1874. However, it should not be forgotten that Gladstone won two of the three elections (1868, 1874 and 1880) which were held under this system. Furthermore, even in 1874 the Liberals obtained an overall majority of the popular vote: they nevertheless lost the election because the reformed electorate was not matched by a reformed distribution of seats, and because of the discrepancy in proportion between large and small constituencies. Thus Disraeli's Reform paid off not because of the triumph of 'Tory democracy', but because the 1867 Act did not reform *enough*, and, in particular, did not reform the counties and the distribution of seats.[3]

Prime Minister

When, in December 1867, Russell informed Gladstone that he would not be prepared to take office again, Gladstone knew that his great opportunity had come. Electoral prospects were very good: the Liberal party had been in office for most of the time from 1830, and the recent electoral reform – despite the fact that it was not the Bill Gladstone would have wanted – promised to produce a new batch of Liberal MPs. On the other hand, at the age of fifty-eight, Gladstone felt old enough to consider his prospective first premiership as his last one.

In the run up to the election all sorts of reform issues were debated by candidates and constituents, depending on their orientation and the special local interests of the constituencies. However, the disestablishment of the Irish Church provided a large common platform on which all branches of the party – from the newly enfranchised radical artisans to the Whig aristocracy – could concur. Predictably, in November 1868 the Liberals won the election, and indeed achieved a majority in each of the three Kingdoms as well as in Wales. Though there were worrying signs of a new vigour in urban Conservatism, there was little evidence that the next twenty years would see a weakening of the Liberal hegemony.

There were lofty expectations as to what the first Parliament elected by borough household franchise would do. Different sections of the Parliamentary party and Liberal movement in the country wanted different things, though all agreed on the basic underlying philosophy. In home affairs, the issues which demanded legislative intervention included the abolition of university tests, reform of the civil service, trade-union law (after the Sheffield outrages and the findings of the Royal Commission); primary education (on whose urgency both radicals and moderates were agreed, though for different reasons), the ballot (a top priority for the radicals) and Ireland, which was a bundle of unsolved problems. Of these areas only the last one commanded Gladstone's unqualified support, while some of the others he regarded with caution, if not open aversion.

Ireland was, of course, one of his old concerns, recently rekindled by the fact that the Emerald Isle was ostensibly the only part of the United Kingdom where the Peelite–Liberal strategy for achieving social peace and economic progress had not worked. There was general agreement within the party that what Ireland needed in the first instance was the abolition of its established Church and the implementation of full religious equality. Disestablishment had a long history in Liberal thought.[4] Since 1834 the Whigs had gradually moved away from the notion of an established Protestant Church in Ireland. By 1867 the legal privileges of the Church were perceived as both anachronistic and unjustifiable in the face of the Catholic and Presbyterian majority of the people. Before retiring from the party leadership Russell had called for both disestablishment and disendowment. In March 1868 this policy was substantially endorsed by Gladstone, who incorporated it in his Irish Church Resolutions. Though the latter were welcomed by Dissenters and Catholics alike, Gladstone's aim was that of strengthening the Irish Church, as much as implementing religious equality. From his own peculiar Tractarian–Evangelical standpoint he felt that the Irish Church itself would benefit from autonomy and freedom from state control, provided it was allowed to retain a substantial proportion of its endowments.[5] The Irish Church Bill was drawn up by Prime Minister himself early in 1869, and given a first reading on 1 March. The only really contentious issue turned out to be the extent of the old endowments which the Irish Church should be allowed to retain – a question eventually settled by compromise.

Disestablishment was Gladstone's first step in his strategy 'to pacify Ireland'. The second step involved land reform. Influential members of the party's left wing – including John Bright and J. S. Mill – insisted that the tenant farmers' lot deserved urgent attention. Though Gladstone did not share their radical views, he agreed on the substance of the matter, and between February 1866 and December 1867 he had discussed an Irish Land Act with his Whig colleague Chichester Fortescue. However, the various pressure groups involved held widely different views: the British radicals wanted the creation of a class of peasant farmers; the Irish Catholic bishops demanded the implementation of the 'Three F's' (free sale, fair rents and fixity of tenure); finally, most of the Whig–Liberal frontbenchers – concerned about the landowners' property rights – found both of these demands utterly unacceptable.

In 1870 Gladstone tried to sail between the Radical Scylla and the Whig Charybdis by proposing a compromise which would offer substantial benefits to the farmers, without affecting the power and authority of the landowners. His proposal was to extend the so-called 'Ulster custom' to the whole of Ireland: this would amount to a substantial increase in tenant rights, involving greater security of tenure and, in the case of eviction, compensation for improvements made to the farm. In its aims this was a typically Peelite reform, which would quell popular unrest without upsetting traditional social relationships. Watered down by the Lords, eventually the 1870 Land Act only sanctioned tenant right in Ulster and offered compensation for improvements in the South. Furthermore, an ineffective 'Bright Clause' (named after the Radical leader) was appended to the Act: it aimed at facilitating land purchase for the tenant farmers who could afford to make use of the rather clumsy and expensive machinery set up by the Act for this purpose. Gladstone insisted that the Act was followed – in 1870 – by the liberation of Fenian prisoners as an act of reconciliation. Yet, because of the moderateness of the land reform, the chance of stabilizing social relations in Ireland had been missed, even if the full extent of the land problem was to become evident only over the next ten years.

Gladstone's third step in his 'pacification' strategy – the reform of university education – proved even more difficult to implement than the first two. The aim of the reform was to 'incorporate' the Irish professional middle class by establishing a fairer university system, free from the old religious biases of Trinity College. In the past separate denominational universities had been established, including Newman's Catholic College (which developed into University College Dublin). While these were poorly endowed, the establishment of the Queen's Colleges, instituted by Peel in 1845, was strongly resisted by the Catholic hierarchy. Gladstone's aim was to establish a 'neutral' university, which would avoid sectarian segregation and embody a new spirit of religious impartiality. From the beginning the Bill attracted strong opposition from both British and Irish MPs, particularly because no theology, philosophy or modern history chairs would be endowed by the state. Yet the Prime Minister was strongly committed to it, and when the Bill was defeated by three votes, on 11

March 1873, the government resigned (only to be forced back into office by Disraeli's refusal to form an alternative administration).

Other measures had greater success, though Gladstone did not play a prominent part in their preparation. The purchase of army commissions was abolished in 1871, first by Royal Warrant, and then by a proper Bill, which the House of Lords accepted only after the Royal Warrant had rendered their position untenable. It was an important step towards the modernization of the British army in the aftermath of the Franco-German War (1870–71), which had established new standards of military professionalism. As for the Ballot Bill, one of the most important steps towards the creation of a more democratic electoral system (especially in Ireland), Gladstone was initially unsympathetic: however, when the Lords rejected the Bill, the Prime Minister supported it and ensured its approval (1872). Similarly, he presided over the drawing of other important Bills, and loyally supported his ministers in Parliament and the country. In contrast to the view that he focused his mind and attention on only one issue at the time, he was in fact able to divide his energy among most of the many Bills, projects and proposals which the government and leading backbenchers produced between 1868 and 1874. Those who knew him intimately were impressed by his stamina. As Goldwin Smith recalled:

> His powers of work were enormous... He once called me to him to help in setting the details of a University Bill. He told me that he had been up over the Bill late at night. We worked at it together from ten in the morning till six in the afternoon, saving an hour and a half which he spent at the Privy Council, leaving me with the Bill. When we parted, he went down to the House, where he spoke at one o'clock the next morning.[6]

Education was an area to which the Liberals devoted much attention with considerable results. The 1869 Endowed Schools Act had a major impact, especially on women's education. However, the most famous, important and difficult social reform passed by the government was the 1870 Education Act. In its final form Forster's Bill proposed to supplement the schools run by the churches by establishing rate-supported schools. The latter were to be managed by local authorities, their boards elected by the ratepayers. Both women and men could vote in the school board elections and stand for office. A form of proportional representation was introduced to ensure that minorities (mainly religious ones, but including women) would have a voice on the new boards. However, while all these features were popular, the religious dimension of the problem proved as intractable as ever.

There were two issues at stake: the first was whether the rate-supported schools should provide religious instruction; the second was whether rate support should be allocated to church schools. The radicals and Nonconformists had hoped that, in its political effects, the Bill would result in a step towards the disestablishment of the Church of England. They wished to undermine Anglican control over the national education system by setting up a competing state system, and by ensuring that the latter would be confined to secular education. In contrast, the Whigs and Conservatives wanted to retain such church control: they saw the Bill as but a device filling the gaps in the existing system, without replacing it. While the former of these two great political differences could be decided locally by the elected school boards, the latter proved unmanageable. The passing of 'Clause 25' (which enabled the boards to fund financially disadvantaged children wishing to attend denominational schools) generated an enormous amount of friction between the Liberal leaders and organized Nonconformity,[7] represented by the powerful National Education League.

Another important area in which the government left its mark was that of trade-union legislation. Gladstone did not play a leading role in this case, though he was well acquainted with the trade-union leaders and admired their businesslike attitude to the labour market.[8] The main problem here had originated with the 'Sheffield outrages' and other similar incidents, uncovered in 1867 by a Royal Commission.[9] These findings and the Commission's final reports had created an urgent need for a redefinition both of the status and privileges of the unions and of the limits within which they could legally engage in strikes. In 1868 the trade unions had, for the first time, elected their congress (the TUC), whose Parliamentary Committee acted as an effective pressure group. The Home Secretary, Bruce, was favourably disposed to its demands, the most important part of which were incorporated into the 1871 Trades Union Act, thus granting full protection for the unions' funds. However, the government needed to respond to the widespread allegations of trade-union 'terrorism' against non-union members, and other criminal activities exposed by the Royal Commission. The TUC agreed that such activities ought to be punished, but rejected 'special' criminal legislation, and feared that the new law could be interpreted to make illegal virtually any activity involved in a strike. No satisfactory solution could be found, and in 1871 an ambiguously worded Criminal Law Amendment Act outlawed picketing in order to protect non-union members (after all, a large majority of the working classes) against intimidation or violence during strikes. However, discussions and meetings between government officials and TUC representatives continued, and by 1873 the new Home Secretary, Robert Lowe, intended to meet the workers' demands along the lines eventually adopted by his Conservative successor, Cross, in 1875. While trade-union legislation and other social reforms have attracted considerable attention among modern historians, at the time these measures were politically non-controversial and non-divisive. Social and economic reforms were generally dealt with in a bipartisan spirit, except when they involved land, drink control or religion (as in the case, respectively, of the 1870 Irish Land Act, the 1872 Licensing Act and the 1870 Education Act).

The Repeal of the Income Tax and the Defeat of 1874

It was on a religious issue that the government had fallen in March 1873. By the end of that year its reconstructed successor was understandably not in good spirits. Gladstone needed an issue on which the party could rejuvenate itself and the government recover its sense of purpose. He thought that financial reform was the question of the future. What he wanted to achieve was something like a renewal of the 'social contract' which had worked so well between 1853 and 1865, but which now required some updating in order to take into account the subsequent social and economic changes and the growing importance and responsibility of local government. By January 1874 the Premier felt able to offer a new plan, which included his famous proposal to repeal the income tax.

The latter represents one of the most controversial projects of Gladstone's career. It is tempting to rationalize it as an attempt to bribe the middle-class electors at the expense of the workers, who reacted by voting either for the Conservatives or not at all. Hence the Liberals' defeat at the election of February 1874. However plausible such an interpretation may appear, it oversimplifies Gladstone's plan, and, as an analysis of the electors' behaviour, it simply does not fit the evidence.

The proposed repeal of the income tax was part of a broad programme of fiscal reconstruction which involved a reform both of central and local taxation. Though the policy of 'remission' of indirect
taxes on the necessities of life would continue (with the planned repeal
of tea and sugar duties), the areas in which reform was urgently needed
were local taxation and the income tax. The former was perhaps the
most immediate and pressing problem, due to the increase in local
government costs through the implementation of urban 'improvement'
schemes and the national education system established by the 1870
Education Act. The burden of local taxation on the working and
lower middle classes became increasingly heavy because of rises in the
rates, which were paid even by the some of the very poor.

As for the income tax, the number of taxpayers had rapidly increased
since 1865, and the category which had increased more than any other
was that of the taxpayers assessed at the lowest level of £100. They were
electorally important: by 1874 they may have comprised about ten
per cent of the registered electors. Moreover, the number of such
poorer income-tax payers was expected to grow further, pushing new
and wider groups above the limit of the £100 exemption. Gladstone
wished to make a fresh appeal to the lower middle classes, which had
formed the rank and file of the Liberal party before 1867, and which
continued to be electorally important. As the previous chapter has
pointed out, in 1853 Gladstone had considered the income tax as a
'temporary' device, a 'wartime' tax to be repealed after the full implementation of free trade. In 1873 he thought that such a time had come.
In order to compensate for the anticipated fall in revenue he intended
to bring about further retrenchment of military expenditure, and
introduce some new tax on property, which would generate a fixed
revenue and could not easily be increased in order to pay for colonial
enterprises and gunboat diplomacy.

Indeed, the chief aim behind the 1874 proposal was that of discour-
aging imperialism and what Gladstone saw as military overspending.
On these issues there were differences between the Prime Minister and
his colleagues in the 'expensive' departments (War, Admiralty and
Colonial Office). One of such differences had come to a head in 1873,
when, virtually against the Premier's will, a 'little war' had been started
in West Africa. Without the income tax – Gladstone reckoned – military
estimates would inevitably become rigid. Rather than some painless
adjustment of a few pence in the pound, special needs would require
the imposition of fresh taxes, always difficult to justify to the electors. As

a result government accountability and financial reform would be fostered.

Thus the 1874 proposed repeal of the income tax served a variety of purposes and would affect the conduct of both home and foreign affairs. It was designed to appeal to the Left without alienating the moderates. It was not a repeal of *all* taxes on income, let alone on property: rather, it aimed at relieving the lower and professional middle classes – which had been overtaxed in comparison with other social groups – by redistributing the fiscal burden on land and real property through local taxation. Gladstone's proposal was in tune with the development of local government responsibility for social reform, and involved the complete transformation of local government, with the establishment of a network of elected authorities throughout the country. It was one of the most ambitious proposals Gladstone had ever conceived – not because of the repeal of the income tax (whose rate was then very low), but because of the other reforms which would have accompanied it.

However, the electors were given little time to either study or understand this elaborate and sophisticated attempt to update the 'social contract'. Dissolution came suddenly and quite unexpectedly. On Saturday 24 January, *The Times* reported Gladstone's decision that the House of Commons would be dissolved immediately. Only then did the Prime Minister reveal his plan for fiscal reform. Within two weeks the first electoral results were announced. Within three weeks the prospect of a Conservative victory was generally established. By contrast, the election of 1868 had been prepared for by the long popular agitation over franchise reform (1865–67), followed by months of discussion of the Irish Question. In 1874 the novelty of the issue before the voters, and the brevity of the electoral campaign meant that Gladstone had little opportunity to deploy one of his chief assets – electoral rhetoric. Virtually no national debate took place. Not surprisingly, the poll was quite poor by Victorian standards, and the comparatively low turnout helped the Conservatives.

In such a situation party machinery and the electoral registers were bound to be the determining factors: and it is well known that the constituency organization of the Liberal party had much deteriorated since 1868, and that the decay of the registers was a universal complaint among Liberal agents. In contrast, thanks to the efforts of Gorst, the Conservative party had raised itself to maximum efficiency and taken particular care in renewing the registers.

From our vantage point Gladstone's tactical mistakes may look surprising, but contemporaries saw things in a different light. Following
the introduction of 'democracy' in 1867 and the secret ballot in 1872,
both parties regarded another Liberal victory as the almost inevitable
outcome of an election under virtually any circumstance. After all, the
Liberals had been the ruling party from 1830, and the 1867 electoral
reform had strengthened their traditional supporters – the Nonconformists, artisans, Irish, Scots and Welsh. What Gladstone really feared was
not a Conservative victory, but internal divisions and the possibility of a
split over the military estimates and colonial policy. By attempting to
carry his programme by a snap election, he wanted to impose his
financial package without openly turning the issue into a political confrontation between 'imperialists' and 'Little Englanders' (it is important
to remember that he did not belong to either group: see Chapter 5).
Had he won – even with a reduced majority – he would have been able
to rule from Number 11 as well as from Number 10 through the
financial restraints implied in his manifesto, a sort of 'fiscal constitution'
(on this concept and its implications see the Appendix to this chapter).
From this point of view, the election was the final master stroke of a
Peelite only half-converted to the demands of the householders'
democracy and the techniques of charismatic leadership.

Appendix

The 'fiscal constitution' is a twentieth-century notion dear to free-
market economists and particularly to the 'Virginia School' of public
finance.[10] In the 1980s writers in this tradition regarded Gladstone as
their hero, and boasted of walking in his footsteps. Indeed, as early as
1931 Henry Neville Gladstone – the premier's eldest son – and the
historian F. W. Hirst appealed to the authority of the 'People's William'
in their crusade against growing state expenditure and social democracy.[11] To what extent are these 'neo-liberal' genealogies historically
legitimate?
    There is no doubt that 'public economy' was a mainstay of Glad-
stone's policy throughout his career, and that towards the end of his life
he expressed his aversion to socialism. However, the context in which
he operated, as well as his background and understanding of the social
and economic reality, were completely different from the context,

background and political agenda of late twentieth-century supporters of the minimalist state. Gladstone lived in a pre-democratic, pre-Welfare era. Throughout most of his long life it was the extreme Left, rather than the Right, that was committed to strict economy in central government expenditure. The 'retrenchment' lobby included not only the 'Manchester School' and intellectuals who followed J. S. Mill, but also veteran Chartists, shrewd cooperators, trade unionists, and republicans like Charles Bradlaugh and, from the 1880s, even the early socialists. In order to understand this apparent paradox we need to bear in mind that at the time both poor relief and education were provided for by local taxation; that virtually no part of central government expenditure was devoted to social purposes; and that much of the revenue was raised through indirect taxes on the 'necessities of life' such as sugar, candles, cloth or corn. In such a context, 'retrenchment' and the accompanying 'remission of taxation' were indeed policies of social concern for which it is difficult to find real equivalents nowadays. Gladstone, like many of the working-class radicals who voted for him, attributed the poverty and social unrest of the post-Waterloo years to the effects that taxation had on popular consumption, the internal market and foreign trade. Protectionism and the corn laws seemed to be the root of the problem.

Moreover, in contrast to Thatcher's centralism, Gladstone's 'minimalist' finance was accompanied by an expanding role for local government, the responsibility and budget of which continued to grow throughout the nineteenth century, and especially from 1870. Thus, while *laissez-faire* and retrenchment were preached at Numbers 10 and 11 Downing Street, 'municipal socialism' was the watchword in town councils and school boards. Local authorities organized various social services under the supervision of central government inspectors and with the help of the loans and 'grants in aid' which Gladstonian surpluses made available. At all levels the principles of *laissez-faire* were applied in a pragmatic way and with due attention to what economists called the 'exceptions' to the principles themselves. These might include the nationalization of 'natural monopolies' like the telegraphs in 1868.

One further important difference between Thatcherite and Gladstonian finance is that, though he was the main architect of Victorian *laissez-faire*, the latter was qualified by his retention of an organicist vision of the state.

4

THE CHARISMATIC LEADER

The Origins of the Charismatic Leader

Most politicians grow more conservative and more cautious as time goes by, moving from youthful idealism to varying degrees of pragmatism after years of exposure to public life. Gladstone moved the other way: a 'stern and unbending' opponent of the 1832 Reform Bill, he lived to champion the vote for the borough artisans in 1864–67, and to enfranchise the farm labourers in 1884–85. Yet in the aftermath of the repeal of the Corn Laws there was little indication that Peel's former Colonial Secretary would display a positive attitude towards franchise reform. Far from showing any sympathy for democratic demands, in April 1848 Gladstone volunteered to serve as a special constable when a Chartist uprising was feared in London. Though the feared revolt turned into the so-called Kennington Common 'fiasco', Gladstone remained unsympathetic to either franchise reform or political radicalism. As late as 1858–59 he had no contact with the forces representing the backbone of popular liberalism, particularly the Nonconformists. Yet the seeds of his populism had already been sown and were beginning to bear fruit.

Inspired by the example of Peel and Aberdeen, Gladstone had developed a specifically Christian (John Vincent has called it 'episcopal')[1] interpretation of the moral obligations of the aristocracy – as a ruling elite – towards the poor. After the Conservative party in his view 'betrayed' Peel in 1846–50, and the middle classes consistently voted for Palmerston's foreign policy in 1853–59, Gladstone concluded that the landed gentry no longer exercised their privileges with Peelite self-denial, while the middle classes were unfit to discharge their electoral duty on behalf of the rest of the country. By contrast, at least from 1862 he was struck by the repeated demonstrations of sympathy and support which he received from artisans and 'respectable' working men. From his Tractarian–Evangelical standpoint he began to reciprocate such feelings. In their humility and simplicity, the working men seemed to him to be close to God and responsive to moral appeals in politics. Strengthened by their (real or imagined) puritanism, they seemed to show a growing responsiveness to Gladstone's calls for financial rectitude and fiscal retribution (see Chapter 2).

Checkland has suggested that Gladstone's admiration for 'the people's' alleged moral virtues was another instance of his tendency to idealize what he was acquainted with only superficially: in his youth he had idealized the Church and the aristocracy; in the 1860s it was the turn of the working classes. After all, '[his] upbringing, unlike that of many of his cousins, had cut him off entirely from any real contact with the masses'.[2] He met them, not as individuals in their ordinary social surroundings, but at open-air demonstrations or in lecture halls – that is, in exhilarating circumstances in which real familiarity was difficult to achieve, and idealization was easy.

When eventually he did develop a closer relationship with some of 'the people', they turned out to be groups of workers, who, however significant, were not 'typical'. They included businesslike trade-union leaders in the 1860s, Nonconformist artisans in 1876 and stern Methodist miners in the 1880s. In each case it was a self-selected audience which gradually substantiated the 'working-class' abstraction in Gladstone's mind: the workers who approached him were precisely those individuals whose lives and inclinations were closest to his ideal. It was like the relationship between a revivalist preacher and his church: the latter was, in a sense, the preacher's own creation. So it was with Gladstone and the working class: though many were called, only the elect came forward, full of enthusiasm and devotion. For him they were models of Christian piety, civic virtue and financial retrenchment. To them Gladstone 'embodied a steadfast and splendid faith, reflected in unshakeable courage. The charisma of the hero-leader was his, combined with that of the saint, needing to consult no one, drawing upon inexhaustible stores of hidden strength'.[3]

However upsetting, the electoral defeat of 1874 gave Gladstone a breathing space at a crucial time in his life. He was now approaching an age at which most other men would consider it normal to retire. Indeed, he did seriously consider doing so. The scholar in him was claiming increasing time and leisure for writing, reading and meditating on his beloved classics. Moreover, he enjoyed his lifestyle as the squire of Hawarden Castle. Thus his decision to sell the London family house and step down from the position of party leader in 1875 (at sixty-five) seemed the prelude to total withdrawal from public life. The party had in Lord Hartington a young and capable leader in the Commons, while Lord Granville upheld the Gladstonian heritage in the Lords. With these two powerful Whigs in commanding positions, his succession was tidily arranged. However, Gladstone retained his Parliamentary seat: sufficient evidence for his former lieutenants to realize that his comeback was a distinct possibility.

Gladstone enjoyed three decisive advantages over his Whig deputies and competitors: political adaptability, a formidable experience and competence as a Cabinet minister and party leader, and, especially, mass-communication skills which were put to good use by a quite a novel type of personal charisma. Moreover, the latter abilities were linked to the most advanced mass media of the time. The telegraph, the railways, the rotative press and cheaper paper (after Gladstone's repeal of the 'taxes on knowledge') made the communication of news and the printing and distribution of newspapers much less expensive. The press had become politically important from the 1850s, when the effects of such technological changes on British politics were enhanced by the impact of a series of spectacular international events, providing a steady stream of exciting news for popular consumption. Both the Crimean War (1853–55) and the struggles of the Italian Risorgimento (1859–61) were widely reported as Liberal crusades against cruel and despicable despots. Between 1861 and 1865, and especially from 1863, the abolitionist campaign during the US Civil War elicited a similar response among British liberals and radicals. Like the Risorgimento, American abolitionism embodied a kind of radicalism which, in contrast to Chartism, was not perceived as socially threatening.

If the Crimea and the Risorgimento had marked the rekindling of popular liberalism after the Chartist debacle of 1848, the Civil War helped to stabilize a British 'popular front' of moral outrage which found a national leader in John Bright. As Asa Briggs has written, John Bright's achievement in 1863–65 was to seize on the universal dimension of the American conflict and link it to the passions, hopes and fears of the common people. Bright identified the issue at stake not as a 'civil' war, but as one between different models of civilization in which the working class of the entire world had a vital interest: the North was fighting a crusade for democracy, liberty and the dignity of labour. In the style of a seventeenth-century radical Puritan, stressing the moral superiority of 'Lazarus' over 'Dives' and the corruption which affects those who trust in material wealth, Bright invested the issue of black emancipation with a character of absolute sacrality, and linked it to his own campaign for the enfranchisement of the British artisans. It was not the case of one class against another, but of humanity against despotism, a cause which he advocated in biblical language combining the Old Testament demand for justice with a New Testament appeal to humanity. In days closer to ours only Martin Luther King has been able to articulate such a 'politics of prophecy' with equal vigour and effectiveness, challenging enemies and supporters alike to reach a higher state of moral awareness.

In many respects Bright's heritage was passed on to and greatly extended by Gladstone. His popularity had been growing steadily throughout the 1860s as a result of his identification with the cause of free trade and fiscal reform. In 1864–67 he reaped the political benefits of his sympathy for reform, and in 1868 his popularity reached a first climax with his introduction of a new dimension into the tradition of popular politics. While Bright stood in the post-Chartist line of the great 'demagogic' outsiders, Gladstone became the first 'people's premier'.

Yet Gladstone's transformation into a populist statesman was not yet completed even by 1875, when he stepped down from the party leadership. In reality his resignation proved to be a turning point in his career. As time went on, the ex-premier's semi-retirement had the effect of eradicating the memory of the disappointments suffered by both Nonconformist and working-class radicals under his leadership, and of enhancing the legend of his triumphs. From 1876 the Bulgarian agitation ensured that the renewal of popular support for liberalism took the form of a personal devotion to Gladstone.

The Bulgarian Agitation, 1876

Devotion is indeed the right word here, for it was a religious spirit that brought Gladstone back to the forefront of national politics. In ideological terms, the burning issue of the day was not dissimilar to that of the Italian Risorgimento: like the Italians fifteen or twenty years previously, in 1875–78 the Bulgarians were fighting for their independence. This could have been sufficient to inspire sympathy and support among British radicals: however, the question was complicated by the fact that imperial power in the Balkans was in the hands of the Ottomans, whose predominantly Muslim armies did not always follow the warfare conventions then commonly accepted in western Europe. When the massacre of large numbers of Christian peasants, of both sexes and all ages, was extensively reported by the *Daily News* and confirmed by *The Times*, the 'Eastern Question' ceased to be one of relevance only to Liberal supporters of oppressed nationalities and became a contest between 'Christian civilization' and 'barbarism', or – as we might say today in a very different idiom – between the advocates of human rights and those perceived as carrying out genocide.[4]

The Bulgarian agitation began spontaneously, with sporadic meetings of protest in northern England. However, it was Gladstone who turned it into a national phenomenon. As Bright before him had done with the abolitionist agitation during the US Civil War, Gladstone seized on the conflict's humanitarian dimension and linked it to the passions, hopes and fears of zealous Nonconformists and pious High-Churchmen. In this context he developed a new relationship with working- and middle-class Nonconformists, becoming the leader of a vast mass movement. Both contemporary observers and the founding fathers of political sociology were deeply impressed by this combination of democratic politics and religious fervour under the leadership of a lay prophet. To the German sociologist Max Weber the post-1876 Gladstone became the prototype of the 'charismatic leader' who – Weber prophesied – would dominate the politics of the twentieth century.

The first example of this new relationship between Gladstone and the crowds was provided by the great open-air meeting held at Blackheath on 9 September 1876, in the wake of the publication of Gladstone's best-selling pamphlet *The Bulgarian Horrors and the Question of the East*. In pouring rain, ten or fifteen thousand people followed Gladstone's exposition with extraordinary enthusiasm. A reporter wrote that, while Gladstone spoke, it was as if the crowd were holding their breath for fear of 'missing their joy': however, every pause in the speech offered an opportunity for voicing their sentiments with shouts of 'Long life to you' and 'We want you.' Gladstone combined his rhetorical skills with the melodramatic ability of a consummate actor or opera singer. Edward Hamilton, Gladstone's secretary, has left one of the most significant accounts:

> His attitude while he was speaking was strikingly dignified and commanding.... There was not a movement of the body that did not give emphasis to the idea he was expressing. The play of his countenance greatly varied; and each variation had its significance. There were looks which were reproachful, sympathetic, and impassioned. Each told its own tale. There were smiles which were at times playful, and at other times almost sardonic. His hawk-like eye was replete with fire. There was great animation and energy in his manner. But most impressive of all was his voice. It was pitched in a middle key. There was a melodiousness about it which hardly could be excelled, if indeed it was ever equalled; and it was used with great dramatic effect. He had an extraordinary power of modulating it. It was always clear when it was subdued; it was never harsh or grating when it was raised to its full power. He could regulate it with as much ease as the organist, skilled in the manipulation of keyboards and stops, can regulate the instrument at which he is sitting. His elocution was extraordinarily clear; while a somewhat peculiar pronunciation of certain words, far from marring his speaking, lent attractiveness to it.[5]

The public was completely absorbed by the personification of concepts and moral imperatives which seemed to be embodied in the orator himself. They 'lived' the speech even before examining its content. 'Mr. Gladstone's personality was more or less suffused among his hearers. It was a kind of hypnotism to which an audience temporarily succumbed'.[6] This was the well-attested phenomenon of 'being Gladstonized'. Part of the secret was that Gladstone's speeches were not written verbatim before the meetings: rather they were constructed *during* the meetings – in a sense, *with* the participation of his audience – from previously composed brief notes. Gladstone himself thus defined oratory:

> The work of the orator, from its very inception, is inextricably mixed up with practice. It is cast in the mould offered to him by the mind of his hearers. It is an influence principally received

from his audience (so to speak) in vapour, which he pours back upon them in a flood. The sympathy and concurrence of his time is [*sic*], with his own mind, joint parent of his work. He cannot follow nor frame his ideals: his choice is, to be what his age will have him, what it requires in order to be moved by him, or else not to be at all.[7]

Even though the impact of Gladstone's rhetoric was overwhelmingly emotional, the content of his speeches was not unrelated to the effect. In this respect his charisma was similar to that of the great Nonconformist preachers of the time: both preacher and sermon were essential components in a sort of drama taking place in an atmosphere of prophetic revelation. The Bulgarian agitation of 1876 followed the Evangelical revivals sparked off all over the United Kingdom by the American evangelists D. W. Moody and I. Sankey, who had visited the British Isles for two years in 1873–75. Since Gladstone – like any typical revivalist preacher – aimed at obtaining acceptance of the 'faith' by his audience, the articles of this 'faith' were an integral part of the evangelistic message. The content contributed towards creating the charisma, and the very language and style of expression helped to define the content. His audience perceived the meetings to be religious occasions, as several autobiographies of working-class radicals testify. Until then only the United States had offered such a mixture of religious values and style, and electoral politics: as early as 1840 William Henry Harrison's presidential campaign had been characterized by a mixture of revivalist style, religious rhetoric and an alliance between American 'Whigs' and Evangelicals. Almost forty years later Gladstone repeated the experiment on a larger scale,[8] transplanting this model of proto-democratic electioneering to Britain. Not surprisingly, American divines were to be found among his greatest admirers. Thus the Revd R. Heber Newton of New York wrote of Gladstone:

One magnificent example of obedience to the heavenly vision is conspicuous in the eyes of the world today. A generation ago a man entered public life in England with the highest possible ideals – ideals which called him to make of statesmanship a service of man, a worship of God. With simple, modest speech he early made it known in Parliament that he looked upon his career not as a promising opening for ambition, not as a field for the political adventurer, but as a lofty mission, a trust from the nation and from the nation's God. He avowed his belief that the supreme work of the State was to promote internal improvements, to ease the burden of labour, to elevate the lot of the masses, to correct abuses, to foster a higher manhood; that international relationships as well as the affairs of individuals were to be brought as far as possible under higher laws; that peace was the true and normal order for Christian nations, and that right and not might should dictate public policy. He came into power and seriously set himself to carry out these principles. He lost power when he moved too straight and steadfast after the heavenly vision of the statesman, for then the people fell away from following after him, and sought other grounds than principle.[9]

Gladstone's hold on the crowd had a markedly charismatic character. Yet, in spite of the presence of such 'irrational' components as his ability to create an emotional form of community relationship, H. C. G. Matthew is right in stressing that the peculiarity of Gladstone's case was that he managed to reconcile mass democracy with the values of traditional liberalism, and formulated a politics which was at the same time charismatic and rational.[10] Matthew has shifted attention from the delivery of Gladstone's speeches to their national dissemination through the press: veneration for the charismatic leader and close attention to and study of the content of his speeches went hand in hand. The latter was a serious business, which took place after the meetings in the workers' homes or in pubs and clubs, where the printed version of the speeches became the subject of long conversations and discussions.

Despite its long, convoluted sentences, Gladstone's prose was highly effective, much more so than the printed version of his speeches would suggest to late twentieth-century readers. It has been said of F. D. Roosevelt that he had the 'talent for explaining complex socio-economic policies in simple but not condescending language'. Something similar could be claimed for Gladstone as well, though he combined the gift with an equally extraordinary ability to make himself ambiguous and mysterious whenever he wanted to keep his options open for possible future changes of policy. This explains why people could respond in such different ways to his oratory, which was sometimes praised for its clarity, and sometimes criticized for its inscrutability. As Edward Hamilton wrote:

Mr. Gladstone combined, in a very marked manner, the power of being perspicuous and the power of being obscure. No one could explain with greater lucidity the provisions of a complicated measure. No one could marshal in clearer array the most minute details. No one could handle in a more luminous fashion figures and statistics, in which he so greatly revelled. And yet, when he wished not to be explicit, and desired to avoid committing himself definitely, no one could be more dexterous in guarding himself, or in wrapping up his meaning in obscure language.[11]

The Midlothian Campaigns

It was during the first two Midlothian campaigns (1879 and 1880) that both the rationalistic and the charismatic components of Gladstone's oratory reached their maximum development. His achievements as a popular leader were then accompanied and rounded off by the emergence of a real 'cult of the leader', which was formally analogous to – though ideologically different from – that which developed in Germany with the socialist Ferdinand Lassalle (1825–64), in France with General Boulanger (1837–91) and Jules Ferry (1832–93), and in Austria with Karl Lueger (1844–1910), the populist mayor of Vienna.

A central component of Gladstone's personality cult became the symbolism of the axe cutting at the root of iniquity. Biblical in origin[12] and also attested both in early nineteenth-century popular radicalism (for example in cartoons on the eve of the 1832 Reform Act) and in democratic and socialist movements, the axe became associated with Gladstone because of his well-known hobby: chopping down sick or dying trees on his estate at Hawarden was a way of combining forest conservation with physical exercise. The imagery of a premier-woodman emphasized what a contemporary observer described as a 'natural homely nature lying behind [Gladstone's] outward unconsciousness of greatness and power'. That this 'homely nature' was an integral part of his charismatic appeal is suggested by an episode which took place in Glasgow. At the end of a speech, while 'the audience went wild with enthusiasm', the statesman's wife stood up from her chair on the platform next to him and began to wipe sweat from 'the great man's face, ears and neck, while he sat back like a young child'. The effect on this unexpected scene on the crowd was immediate and powerful: 'Their [i.e. the Gladstones'] complete forgetfulness of the enthusiastic audience touched everyone, and the whole place was overcome with emotion. The cheering died away, and in all parts of the hall one could see handkerchiefs as the members of the audience wiped their tear-filled eyes.'[13] This anecdote also provides an example of the importance of the women in Gladstone's entourage for the building of his myth: another 'American' feature of his charisma, at the time (and for a long time since, until Tony Blair's wife, Cherie) quite unusual in Britain.

Such was the extent of the empathy between Gladstone and his popular followers that veneration and familiarity were closely intertwined. Perhaps few went so far as walking more than ten miles to present home-made butter and eggs to 'dear Mr. Gladstone', as did an old countrywoman at the 1876 Blackheath meeting; but cases like that of James Hawker, the Leicestershire poacher who kept a photograph of the 'People's William' in his diary, must have been quite common. While in some regions of Germany and Italy it was usual for workers to choose names like 'Lassalle' and 'Marxina' for their children, in Britain there was a proliferation of 'William Ewarts'. It is certain that both veneration and familiarity were implicit in the appellation 'Grand Old Man' (or G.O.M.), apparently coined by Shaw Lefevre in 1881 and rapidly adopted by the popular weekly press and pamphlet writers.

During the Midlothian campaigns Britain was witness to political scenes which were as yet unknown on the eastern shores of the Atlantic. Gladstone's electoral campaigns and his effectiveness in bringing a political message to the masses had overtaken any continental European model. In his analysis of contemporary American democracy, Moisei Ostrogorski wrote that the aim of rhetoric was the winning of those who are indifferent, and to influence the greatest possible number: '[a]ppealing even to the lowest strata of the electorate, who can hardly be reached by print, the meetings, in fact, do succeed in attracting electors of every degree'.[14] By this standard Gladstone's success was remarkable: newspaper reports record that even women and children mingled with the excited crowds in the stations and streets, striving to shake hands with the Liberal leader. Miners left their pits and labourers their ploughs to line up along the railway tracks in the open countryside, and greet the train on which they knew that Gladstone was travelling: yet it was hardly possible for them to see him, not so much because of the speed at which the train passed, but because the People's William, in his compartment, would be busy dictating his latest speech to the reporters who accompanied him. Contemporary reports show not only the widespread extent of Gladstone's popularity, but also his capacity for engendering enthusiasm throughout the several regions along the route of his electoral travels.

Between November–December 1879 and March–April 1880 hundreds of thousands of people listened to at least one of Gladstone's speeches and were directly influenced by him, as is evidenced by the fact that the Liberals gained a seat at every stop where he had spoken. But his fascination reached well beyond the regions that he visited, and daily throughout the country millions of people followed his precise, hammering rhetoric in the reports published in all newspapers – both Liberal *and* Conservative. The climax of his influence came during the famous 'Midlothian campaigns', the first of which was begun in 1879 and led, in April 1880, to Gladstone's election as MP for the Scottish constituency of that name, and, many argued, was instrumental in bringing about the nationwide defeat of the Conservative party. Historians have questioned the extent to which the 'Midlothian campaign' was actually effective in winning the election; however, people at the time had little doubt that Gladstone was the chief architect of the Liberal victory and the only man who could form a cabinet. Despite the hostility of the Queen, who disliked Gladstone at least as much as she liked Disraeli, the 'People's William' was asked to form his second government in 1880 (the only time a non-party leader has become Prime Minister).

Though it is often compared unfavourably with the 1868–74 government, Gladstone's second premiership (1880–85) was more successful than his first one from the point of view of his capacity for preserving popular support and party unity. For example, he retained total control of the party while implementing his new Irish legislation, which combined advanced land reform (hated by the Whigs) with severe coercion measures (anathema to the Radicals). Even the controversial invasion of Egypt in 1882 – in direct contradiction of his electoral pledges – found many advocates among his popular following, and had the benefit of a substantial silent complicity even from those who were usually inflexible anti-imperialists, with the sole exception of John Bright. Later, he rode roughshod through the Sudan imbroglio[15] – which generated military commitments more expensive than anything Disraeli had done – and the party still followed him when he asked for a special Vote of Credit to ward off Russia in Afghanistan in 1885. As a critic bitterly pointed out,

He has shaped Liberal policy according to his own will, and Liberals throughout the country have been expected to admire, applaud, and acquiesce. Does he decree coercion for Ireland? Then in the eyes of the Liberals coercion is no longer a crime, but a necessity, and almost a virtue. Does he bombard and destroy Alexandria, ruthlessly suppress the national movement in Egypt, and banish Arabi the Patriot? Then these acts of arbitrary repression and wanton destruction lose their cruelty and injustice. Does he squander millions of British gold and spill blood like water in the deserts of the Soudan? Every Liberal leader, writer and platform orator at once discovers that war and waste are iniquitous only when done by Tories, and ministers of the Gospel who are Liberals subordinate the precepts of Christ to the policy of W. E. Gladstone. . . . Party spirit and loyalty to Mr. Gladstone seemed to completely invert the ideas of many excellent men on the simplest and most palpable questions of right and wrong. Their leader was not to be bound even by the moral law; he was regarded as being above that law; he was a law unto himself. While Mr. Gladstone was waging some of the most wanton wars of this generation, he was being extolled by Christian (?) journals for his 'passionate love of peace'.[16]

Paraphrasing a common expression, it could be said that the accepted opinion among many electors was 'our William, right or wrong'. The long campaign for the 1884 Franchise Reform Bill came at just the right time to reinvigorate rank-and-file Liberalism and renew the cult of the G.O.M. During those months other statesmen received enthusiastic receptions at Liberal meetings: but nobody else was able to sustain a relationship with the masses similar to that firmly established by Gladstone. It is a striking fact that by then the intimacy between the G.O.M. and the workers had apparently increased, though he was now premier and had been in office for four long and difficult years. Not only were the usual frantic scenes and continuous celebrations repeated, but also the press reported a number of short dialogues between Gladstone and his admirers, in what contemporaries and modern sociologists alike have described as a 'choral form', with audiences – like church congregations – joining in the praise of the leader at appropriate intervals, and after much communal singing.

However, in 1884 as much as in previous campaigns Gladstone reached the apex of his political effectiveness during the great mass

meetings, when he addressed long and elaborate speeches to the newspaper readership as much as to the local audience. Up to 15,000
workers congregated to listen to the G.O.M. in the Waverley Market
Hall, at Edinburgh, in September 1884. Among the decorations in the
hall were remarkable elements which would have been familiar to a
reporter of Lassalle's socialist meetings in Germany: items such as the
flags of the local trade unions hanging from the ceiling, together with
portraits of 'the leader'. On the whole the scene symbolized the 'fusion'
between organized labour movement and charismatic leader, and,
through the latter, the integration of the trade unions into the Liberal
party. A hypothetical German observer would also have been struck by
other similarities to socialist meetings in the *Kaiserreich*, and especially
by the fact that 'the entrance of the leader' had become the moment of
highest collective exaltation. As in Ferdinand Lassalle's Rhineland, so in
Midlothian, the leader's entrance provided impressive evidence of the
movement's unity and of the extent to which it was personified in him.
Contemporary British critics, anticipating the pessimism of a later
generation of German sociologists, voiced their growing concern
about the potential constitutional dangers associated with this rise of a
'cult of the leader':

> We are told by some of our instructors that the hope of modern
> nations is in one-man government; that it is only under such a
> system of government that there is any chance of having a vigorous
> policy; that the multitudes love to worship a political idol – that they
> are at heart hero-worshippers; and that even Democracies would
> rather be misled by a man whom they trust than take the responsi-
> bilities of finding their way themselves. This is false and deceitful
> philosophy, and cannot be too strongly reprobated by all friends of
> progress. If Democracy is merely to land us in Caesarism; if all men
> are to be enfranchised only in order that they may bow their knee to
> one man; then those who believe in freedom and progress are
> deluded.... [17]

The implied comparison was between Gladstone and Bismarck:[18]
allegedly the British were just as abject and servile in their worship of
the G.O.M. as the Germans were in their attitude to the Iron Chancellor. However, a better parallel could have been offered by American
democratic politics. If one reads reports of Republican and Democrat
conventions in the United States in the 1890s, it is easy to recognize

features with which Britain was by then more than familiar. During the
Midlothian meetings all the paraphernalia of American electoral politics were in place. The similarities included – besides the display of flags
and portraits of the leader – the large numbers of people involved,
their enthusiasm, aroused by the use of songs and hymns, and the role
of prayers at crucial times. In Britain as much as in America one of the
chief attractions 'for the crowd that cares little for political eloquence
consists of interludes executed by orchestras and choruses'.[19] This
technique was adopted also by the organizers of Gladstonian meetings.
At the Manchester Free Trade Hall during the 1886 electoral campaign, while waiting for the G.O.M. 'a pink programme of music was
sown broadcast among the audience. ... The organ was played and the
vast audience whiled away the time in singing right vigorously a series
of songs, mostly in praise of the Premier' (*Daily News*, 26 June 1886).
Some of these hymns have survived on an 1885 song sheet. They
contained words like the following (to the tune of 'Bonnie Dundee'):

> To the millions of England 'twas Gladstone who spoke
> 'I've freed you at last from the Squires' strong yoke,
> The march of the people to triumph I've led,
> And henceforth the rule of the Tories is dead.
>
> Come, follow me, men, for the fight that is near;
> Come, gather and rank for the battle that's here;
> And again your old Leader to lead you you'll see,
> And you'll fight and you'll conquer again led by me.

Another hymn (on the air: 'March of the Men of Harlech') concluded:

> Gladstone's government shall rule us,
> Men like these will lead, not school us,
> Tory tricks no more shall fool us,
> We've a better way!
> Equal rights all shall be sharing,
> Equal burdens all be bearing;
> Each for all, for all each caring –
> Hail the happy day!

The final hymn on the sheet was to the rousing tune of 'Auld Lang
Syne', and proclaimed, among other things,

In Gladstone still, 'the People's Will,'
Strong hand, brave heart, combine
To send Lib'ral breasts a thrill, as in days of auld lang syne.

Such songs had three basic themes: the centrality of the leader, his
past achievements and the close relationship – a brotherhood in arms –
between leader and led. By then the style of Gladstonian meetings had
reached American standards, and, consciously or unconsciously, was
reminiscent of presidential campaigns.

'Masses Versus Classes'

Though Gladstone was no democrat – indeed, he always remained a
patrician who believed in the aristocratic principle in government – he
became both a leader of democrats and an icon for those who loathed
the landed gentry. But, however extraordinary, his political evolution
was not unparalleled: indeed, the history of politics involves a long
tradition of patrician 'demagogues', stretching from Pericles, the Grac-
chi and Caesar to Theodore and F. D. Roosevelt, Winston Churchill
and J. F. Kennedy. It is not usual for aristocrats to be willing leaders of
crusades against their own order, as allegedly Gladstone was in the late
1880s; but some – like Gladstone's contemporary and colleague C. S.
Parnell[20] – believed that the best way for the aristocracy to preserve
power was to initiate change themselves. Gladstone's strategy was not
dissimilar: he sought not an overhaul of aristocratic society, but its
'moralization', its updating so that it could better face the challenges
of democracy. Paraphrasing Lionel Tollemache, we could conclude that
'the English Government under [Gladstone's] guidance might be compared to the Athenian Government under the guidance of Pericles: "it
was nominally a democracy, but in reality the supremacy of the first
citizen[s]." '[21]
As Colin Matthew and Boyd Hilton have suggested, Gladstonian
political reform was really applied Peelism cum Aristotelian political
'virtue' in a Christian guise. Neither is this evolution difficult to explain
in Gladstone's own terms. In principle, Gladstone pursued stability, not
change. In practice, he realized that stability could be achieved only by
establishing a greater degree of justice and equity, and that this
required political and economic reform. Thus, import duties had to

be abolished in order to give free rein to the natural balancing tendencies in the market; taxation had to be redistributed in order to
stimulate productivity and employment; the franchise had to be low-
ered in order to liberate the forces of stability and progress embodied
in working-class householders; Ireland had to be given a separate
Parliament in order to empower the natural sense of responsibility
among both Irish politicians and electors, and to lighten the burdens
of the Imperial Parliament. In all these instances his aim was the
'restoration' of a self-acting mechanism requiring no further external
intervention. However, the cumulative effect of all such 'restorative'
measures was to turn Gladstone – in practice though not in principle –
into a 'conservative radical', or even, as he was often perceived, into a
radical Liberal.

In appealing to the 'masses' against the 'classes' Gladstone alienated
much of the political centre and tantalized the Left. Yet, to him the
language of 'masses' versus 'classes' did not mean anything like the
modern 'class struggle', but, on the contrary, a reassertion of traditional
political values such as 'civic virtue' and 'public interest' against what he
saw as irresponsible privilege. The 'classes', especially the metropolitan
rentiers, whether aristocrats or bourgeois, were those who had supported Beaconsfield's 'reckless' foreign policy in 1876–80, and opposed
Home Rule for Ireland in 1886–94. They were 'evil' not because they
were wealthy, but because – Gladstone argued – they were animated by
a sectional spirit rather than public interest.

From 1884, after his confrontation with the House of Lords over the
Franchise Bill, Gladstone was forced to move increasingly closer to
the masses as the only reliable basis for a 'virtuous' citizenry. They
were the 'non-class' nation, whether provincial Nonconformist middle
classes or organised working men. Even while the early socialist organizations began to disseminate their ideology, Gladstone showed little
sensitivity to class struggle as a political factor, but continued to see class
in purely negative terms. He insisted that such sectional concerns
should not be allowed to stand in the way of public interest. In this
respect his views were consonant with the tradition of Aristotelian
'republicanism', the classical notion of citizenship as a matter of duty
to the 'common wealth', or *res publica*.

Among historians and political theorists nowadays there is a tend-
ency to forget the extent to which not only Gladstone, but the whole of
Victorian Liberalism was informed by values that Quentin Skinner and
John Pocock have identified as 'the Machiavellian moment' of north

Atlantic political culture.[22] Yet both Gladstone and most of his ministers
– such as W. E. Forster, A. J. Mundella, and Lord Spencer – saw
participatory citizenship as a crucial Liberal value: such view was notor-
iously shared by the main political thinkers of the time, including John
Stuart Mill, Thomas Hill Green and Alfred Marshall. Civic magistracies
and active involvement in the 'citizens' army' (the Volunteers movement) or local government were prized as schools of civic virtue. Thus,
speaking in Dublin in November 1877, Gladstone praised Birmingham
municipal politics, not because he approved of the ambitious social
reforms carried out by the corporation, but because they fostered an
'active spirit of public discussion and government, and attracted the
best citizens to municipal service':

> No one...can visit that town without being struck by the extraor-
> dinary energy that pervades the whole of the institutions and the
> whole of the public life of the place. The consequence is that men
> have their own peculiar opinions and entertain them freely; but
> with regard to one another they do not attempt to coerce one
> another. They resent and have put down all class ascendancy and
> class interests are not known in the municipal elections. And what is
> the result? They have in that town the best men to fill their public
> places.[23]

Remarkably, his eulogy was (perhaps consciously?) reminiscent of
Pericles' celebrated 'Funeral Speech', that classical statement of 'civic
virtue liberalism' with which Victorian schoolboys would have been
familiar, either in Thucydides' original or in George Grote's translation.
Thus, far from pursuing 'working-class' support in the socialist sense of
the term, Gladstone aimed at integrating working-class householders in
to his classless, civic-minded vision of politics, within which they were
expected to operate neither as a class nor as individuals, but as citizens
with duties to the state.

Nevertheless, Gladstone paid a high political price for his ability to
muster the working-class electorate. As the Irish nationalist T. P. O'Connor observed in 1885,

> He is not loved by the Whigs; he is loathed by many of the
> Tories. The infinite subtleties of his extraordinary mind, the infinite
> resources of his boundless rhetoric, appear to many of them only
> the mean devices of a tricky and unscrupulous gambler with

truth, and the fervid passion which he throws into his speeches...ex-
cites in his opponents anger as hot as his own appears to be. The
Tories distrust and fear Mr Gladstone, and Mr Gladstone lashes and
envenoms the Tories. The Whigs, on the other hand...dread Mr
Gladstone's impulsiveness, changeableness, and dangerous tendency
to be heated by the popular fire which he himself is so able to kindle.
All these enmities to Mr Gladstone are, of course, submerged when
the tide of his popularity and strength runs high, and bitter enemies
join with devoted friends in slavish lip-service.[24]

To be sure, his charisma could not always carry the day. While the
party rhetoric signalled a steady move leftwards, underscored by franchise extension and land reform, the Whig landed aristocracy felt
positively alienated. Thus, the Duke of Argyll resigned over the 1881
Irish Land Bill, finding it hardly compatible with property rights and
the interests of the landed elite. Other grandees soon followed suit,
despite Gladstone's efforts to reassure and keep them in his party. But
most Whigs could only give a reluctant assent to policies which were
increasingly becoming too 'democratic' for their tastes.

The crisis came, quite predictably, over Irish issues in 1886, when
Gladstone adopted a policy of Home Rule. Lord Hartington's refusal to
join and the secession of many Whigs were the inevitable outcome of
the radicalization of the Liberal party, especially at a time when an
attractively moderate Conservative party was effectively tackling the
issue of imperialism, which – in the age of the 'scramble for Africa' –
had a powerful emotional appeal on large sections of the electorate.

5

FOREIGN POLICY AND THE EMPIRE

The Financial Constraints of Liberal Policy

There are many reasons why Gladstone could not sympathize with the new imperialistic frame of mind which became so influential from the 1880s. As we have seen, the opportunity for a comeback after the 1874 electoral debacle arose as a result of the Eastern Question in 1876–80, when he found himself at the head of a mass protest movement against Beaconfield's handling of the Eastern crisis. Yet it should not be forgotten that, even more than the Tories' foreign and imperial policy, it was their management of the Exchequer which attracted Gladstone's criticism. And it is important to bear in mind that foreign and financial policies were reciprocally interdependent.

Between 1874 and 1880 Disraeli (Lord Beaconsfield from 1876) presided over a government which is justly remembered as one of the most effective in the nineteenth century. However, its administration of public finance and taxation was not popular at the time. Part of the problem was, of course, conjunctural: having taken office at the onset of the so-called 'Great Depression' (1874–96), the Conservatives then had to contend with a set of new problems, such as a steady fall in revenue, recurrent trade crises and rising unemployment. Furthermore, the deterioration of international relations, combined with tedious and expensive colonial wars, meant that military expenditure had to be maintained at higher levels than in previous periods. From 1876 there were deficits in the ordinary budget, with occasional supplementary budgets to provide for military involvement in the continuing imperial crises.

Not only did Gladstone disagree with Beaconsfield's analysis of Britain's commitments overseas, but he also disapproved of the way his government tried to provide for the costly implications of such commitments. In contrast, Gladstone insisted that peacetime finance ought to respect the four Peelite principles of retrenchment, rationalization of state expenditure, the production of balanced budgets, and the reduction of the national debt. By 1876 he had reached the conclusion that the Conservatives, while doing nothing at all about the redemption of the debt, were more or less neglecting the other three rules as well.

This criticism was hardly fair to Disraeli's Chancellor – Sir Stafford Northcote – considering the special problems that he had to face. Indeed, some modern historians have tried to defend the Conservative policy of expanding the Debt rather than increasing taxation as one more suited to times of trade crisis and unemployment than Gladstone's financial austerity and emphasis on 'paying the country's way'. However, there are two basic problems with this 'proto-Keynesian' interpretation: first, state expenditure at the time represented such a small fraction of the gross national product that its effects on the economy would not have had any counter-cyclical consequences. Second, the government's running of a series of deficits had negative psychological effects on the business community – including the TUC, which was becoming increasingly nervous as unemployment began to affect even skilled labour. In all quarters, and despite Disraeli's social reforms and showy foreign policy, nostalgia for the old style of financial administration was stimulating a Liberal reaction.

Thus, during the Midlothian campaigns of 1879–80 (see Chapter 4), Gladstone exploited effectively the government's failure to meet accepted standards of financial management. Though such principles had been established during decades of extraordinary economic expansion (1850–73), their general validity was not challenged by Gladstone's opponents. As a consequence the Tories' financial strategy only looked weak and irresolute. It was widely held that the chief reason for their inability to raise the necessary revenue to meet the cost of their 'reckless' foreign policy was that they feared the electoral consequences of increased taxation. Thus they were represented as lacking the courage of their own convictions – an 'irresponsible and profligate' behaviour which Gladstone denounced with devastating effect.

At the election popular dissatisfaction and frustration resulted in a landslide Liberal victory. As we have seen, this success, widely perceived as Gladstone's personal triumph, allowed the 'People's William' to resume the party leadership and manoeuvre his colleagues into offering him the premiership. On assuming office he took upon himself the additional responsibility of Chancellor of the Exchequer. Such a combination of tasks would have been unusual for a younger politician, but was quite extraordinary for a 72-year-old statesman.

The new government had two top priorities, and success in achieving the one depended on its ability in securing the other: the first was the restoration of financial 'rectitude', and the other was the pacification of both Europe and the frontiers of the British Empire. Peace abroad would allow for retrenchment at home. At first it seemed that Gladstone would be able to redeem his pledge, the repeal of the Malt Tax in 1880 being a considerable success. However, from 1882, accumulated debts, compounded by fresh financial burdens, contributed towards making traditional retrenchment hardly feasible. The new military commitments in the Transvaal and Egypt (see below, pp. 78, 85–9), knocked down two of the pillars of classical Gladstonianism: 'Peace' and 'Retrenchment'. In a speech in 1883 Gladstone tried to rationalize his predicament by comparing the situation with the one he had to face at the beginning of his career: he argued that, once the expenses for tax collection, grants-in-aid and the war in Egypt had been deducted, the difference in the 'net' expenditure in 1840 and that in 1882 was a modest increase of 34 per cent – from £47,275,000 to £62,955,000 (in 1882 the *gross* expenditure was £88,906,000). Incidentally, over the same period grants-in-aid (relief of ratepayers, mainly for education and other social purposes) increased from £620,000 to over £6 million.[1] The problem with this reasoning was, of course, that neither the grants-in-aid (and social expenditure in general), nor the colonial wars and the related increased military estimates were episodic or 'exceptional' expenses: they both would continue to rise during the next thirty or forty years, requiring ever greater allocation of state funds. In 1884 Gladstone listed the main and most intractable sources of expenditure under three headings:

First of all there has been a natural and normal growth of certain charges – a desirable growth of certain charges – such as the education vote. The education vote grows rapidly from year to year; and who is there among the thousands I address that

would wish to check its growth?...[Second, there] was the great
increase of charge in the civil government of Ireland; but
[third] I do not hesitate to say this, that the main cause which
has kept the expenditure of the country so high has been the
~~military charge~~, which was mainly, if not entirely, due to the
policy of the foregoing Government, and the engagements with
which they had saddled those who had succeeded them.[2]

Yet the Liberal government continued to become involved in expensive military enterprises. In fact, in 1885 the crisis in Sudan – where a
British expeditionary force was engaged in a desperate fight against
Islamic fundamentalists in their unsuccessful attempt to relieve Gordon
at Khartoum – and the danger of a new major war in Afghanistan in
order to contain the recently revived Russian expansionism (the Pend-
jeh crisis), meant that 'retrenchment' had to be abandoned altogether.
In dealing with the Tsar, Gladstone displayed a moderation in aims but
firm resolve in means. This resulted in a compromise which made
possible to avoid a potentially disastrous war with the Russian Empire.[3]
However, for the Liberal government the immediate result of the
Afghan crisis was defeat in Parliament and loss of office: the increased
estimates for the necessary military preparations were the last straw for
its tired and embattled majority. It was over a £100 million budget that
the government lost the crucial vote on 8 June 1885. It was ironic that
Gladstone's second government, when the G.O.M. ruled unchallenged,
saw financial policy being dictated by external affairs and military
concerns.

Europe

How could such a disaster (in Gladstonian terms) have come about? As
we have seen in Chapter 3, in 1874 Gladstone had sought to impose a
'fiscal constitution' on the defence departments. This had long been his
dream. While serving as Palmerston's Chancellor of the Exchequer
(1859–65) he had tried, with limited success, to produce financial policies which would restrain expenditure on external affairs, a Cobdenite
strategy which had paved the way for a closer relationship with the
Radicals. Indeed Gladstone had drawn closer to Cobden in 1850,
when they had jointly opposed Palmerston's bullying of Greece (the

Don Pacifico case). Their alliance was further consolidated later in 1858, when they both spoke out against British gunboat diplomacy in China (the so-called *Arrow* incident, leading to the second 'opium war'). It was then that Gladstone appealed, for the first time, to the 'sisterhood among nations' and their rights, irrespective of power or size.

Although Gladstone's view of international law was sustained by his Christian faith and his rhetoric inspired by moral concerns, there was a strict interdependence between his philosophy of international relations and his views of financial policy. Both were inherited from the Peel government, whose foreign secretary, Lord Aberdeen, had been Gladstone's mentor. Aberdeen personified the connection between 'Peace', 'Retrenchment' and the preservation of the 'Concert of Europe'. The latter was, originally, a conservative system derived from the 1815 Vienna settlement. Based on the notion of collective responsibility, its aim was the avoidance of full-scale conflict by means of consultation among the five big powers – Britain, France, Austria, Prussia and Russia – whose representatives would meet periodically at congresses and conferences. These countries were prepared to put diplomatic and military pressure on troublemakers, for the preservation of the balance of power and a Christian-inspired 'international law'. The latter had originally been understood in strictly conservative terms in the days of the 'Holy Alliance'. However, especially under Canning, Britain had successfully modified such an interpretation. After 1830 the establishment of a more liberal regime in France allowed for the development of an ideologically inspired 'western alliance' between London and Paris. This worked effectively on behalf of liberal revolutionaries in Belgium, Spain and Portugal, without significantly altering either the workings or legitimacy of the 'Concert'. After 1851 Napoleon III, though often unpredictable and generally distrusted, remained loyal to the system, which was reinstated during the Crimean War and ensuing Paris Congress of 1856.

The first major challenge to the European balance of power came in 1859–60, with Italian unification, though without producing any drastic modification of the system. United Italy was not a real power, and Cavour, like other European liberal diplomats, valued the 'moral consortium' among governments more than abstract theories of nationality: he saw it as the counterpart to his free-trade dream of an ordered and rational progress, sustained by both foreign and national investments. Thus, when we consider British attitudes to the Italian case we must always bear in mind the liberal–conservative nature of the

Risorgimento, as a movement stabilizing not only the internal affairs of the peninsula, after decades of upheavals and rebellions, but also the international affairs of Europe.

Indeed, Palmerston had envisaged a settlement along similar lines as early as 1848, when British diplomacy was deployed to support the Piedmontese liberals against both Austrian reactionary intentions in Lombardy, and French Republican designs on Savoy and Nice. Of course, even though Palmerston favoured the creation of a north Italian state under the Piedmontese constitutional monarchy – a sort of Italian Belgium – he was not interested in Italian unification. Thus in 1859 he tried unsuccessfully to prevent the outbreak of the Franco-Austrian war in northern Italy, the possible outcome of which, he feared, would lead to the dismemberment of the Austrian empire and to French hegemony in Central Europe and the Mediterranean. However, in 1859–61 Napoleon III, Cavour and Garibaldi – an unlikely trio – more or less unwittingly squared the circle of British Liberal dreams: though each of the three sought territorial expansion by means of secret treaties, war and revolution, they were prepared to operate within the confines of the European balance of power. As a consequence Austria was expelled from the Po valley; France had to content itself with very moderate territorial expansion in Nice and Savoy (sanctioned by local referenda); the Pope lost most of his territories; and Italy was unified, but on terms uniquely favourable to British interests in the Mediterranean. Palmerston played the international moralist on the cheap, and his government reaped where others had sown. Of course, this strategy – if such it can be called – did not always work out: in 1864 Palmerston committed British support to another constitutional monarchy, Denmark, but when the latter was attacked by Prussia and Austria his bluff was called. Britain was in no position to engage in a continental war: the Danes were defeated, and lost Schleswig-Holstein to the German Confederation.

We may wonder whether this combination of liberalism and pragmatism was superseded by a more idealistic approach once Palmerston was replaced by Gladstone as Liberal party leader and Prime Minister. The answer is that this change affected rhetoric and ideology more than the actual conduct of foreign affairs. The latter continued to be motivated by cautious pragmatism and concern for British imperial interests. There were undoubtedly differences of style and outlook between the two statesmen, highlighted by Gladstone's warm reception of Garibaldi – whose name was then a byword for democratic revolution – during the General's visit to London in 1864.[4] Moreover, Gladstone personified a high-minded Christian approach in international relations as much as he did in home affairs, and he had often criticized Palmerston's policies. On the other hand, Gladstone was genuinely appreciative of Palmerston's liberalism, which he defended in private conversations as late as 1896. He argued that 'Palmerston had two admirable qualities. He had an intense love of Constitutional freedom everywhere; and he had a profound hatred of negro slavery.'[5] Furthermore, as we saw in Chapter 1, Gladstone's final 'conversion' to Liberalism had taken place between 1851 and 1859, over the Italian issue, on which his views were similar to Palmerston's.

Gladstone, like Palmerston, was not a pacifist, and under certain circumstances was ready to sanction the use of force. Thus, in 1859–60, after an initial period of indecision, he supported the unification of Italy, though it involved war, revolution and the end of the Vienna Congress settlement. Generally, however, his approach was one which allowed for the peaceful (and economical) change and the enforcement of international treaties, as exemplified by his response to the three international crises of 1870–71. These involved Britain's relations with, respectively, Germany and France, Russia and the USA.

At the beginning of the Franco-Prussian war, Gladstone took active steps to preserve the independence of Belgium: had its neutrality been violated by either France or Germany, Britain – he said – would fight for Brussels. This policy was not dissimilar to Palmerston's stand on Schleswig-Holstein in 1864, but followed a much longer tradition in British politics. In particular, in 1839 the British government had guaranteed Belgian neutrality, and in 1848 Palmerston had made it clear to the French Revolutionary government that an invasion of Belgium would have been a *casus belli* for Britain.[6]

Belgian neutrality was not violated in 1870, but Gladstone was unable to prevent the Germans from annexing Alsace and Lorraine against their inhabitants' will in 1871. He then tried to persuade the cabinet to make an official protest. When his attempt failed, he took an unprecedented step for a British Prime Minister and published an anonymous article in the *Edinburgh Review*, condemning Bismarck's annexation and celebrating Britain's fortunate insularity, protected as it was by 'a streak of silver sea'.[7] More successful was Gladstone's Russian policy, when he prevailed upon the government of St Petersburg to come to the negotiating table, rather than unilaterally to break the Black Sea Clauses of the 1856 Paris Treaty.

Finally, Gladstone managed to settle by international arbitration the Anglo-American dispute over the losses inflicted on US shipping by British-built Confederate cruisers during the American Civil War. This was the famous *Alabama* case, named after one of the privateering warships. Eventually a specially convened international court ruled that the British government owed £3,250,000 as reparations to Washington, and Gladstone agreed to pay (typically, he asked for a cash discount in return for an immediate payment). Though his 'surrender' to foreign judges and Yankee bullying was criticized bitterly both by jingo opinion at the time and by some historians since, the peaceful resolution of this problem was a great success for the British Empire. At the very least the settlement prevented an escalation of tension which might have caused long-term problems in Anglo-American relationships. In the worst scenario, it averted an armed conflict: and it was evident at the time that, in the event of a war, the scant British forces in North America – thinly deployed along the Canadian frontier – would have been no match for the Civil War veterans of the US army. Furthermore, the likely expense of a full-scale war, not to mention the difficulty of protecting other British dependencies overseas against American naval incursions, simply bore no comparison with the settlement cost paid out by the Liberal government after arbitration. But to Gladstone what was most important was the principle thus established – namely, that international conflicts between Christian powers could be settled without recourse to force of arms.

This attitude was further illustrated in 1876. Gladstone's Christian faith played a particularly important role in shaping the course of actions adopted during the Eastern crisis. As a High-Churchman, he recognized the Eastern Orthodox Church as a legitimate 'national' branch of the universal Church of Christ. He drew a parallel between the unity of Christendom and that of the Concert of Europe. If there ought to be co-operation, reciprocal support and 'joint action' among the various national branches of the Church, the same rule should be followed by the governments which these churches sought to guide. In 1876, as Gladstone's Christian sense of the 'unity of Europe' bred what has appropriately been described as his 'cosmopolitan patriotism',[8] his High-Church reasoning coincided with the Evangelical humanitarian-ism of the Nonconformists. The old alliance between the 'People's William' and the earnest Dissenters was thus renewed on issues of foreign policy.

Gladstone's campaign against the methods and strategies adopted by Lord Beaconsfield was intensified in 1877–80, when, as we have seen, he focused attention on a new series of expensive blunders (which he branded as crimes) committed by the Tory administration and their colonial proconsuls. He concentrated on the difficult wars in South Africa (against the Zulus) and Afghanistan, as well as on the recent expansion in the Mediterranean. The latter involved the occupation of Cyprus and the purchase of shares in the Suez Canal, both of which he feared would be the prelude to an ever-growing British involvement in North Africa. At the time he considered the Egyptian move as strategically pointless: 'Suppose the very worst. The Canal is stopped. And what then? ... It seems to be forgotten by many that there is a route to India round the Cape of Good Hope.'

In Midlothian, in 1879, he outlined an alternative foreign policy, based on six principles which would 'form a landmark in the history of Liberal internationalism'.[9] These included both commitment to the preservation of the peace, and to strengthening the Concert of Europe as the arbiter and arena for the peaceful solution of international conflicts, and respect for the peoples's right of self-determination. To Disraeli's Latin motto of *Imperium et Libertas*, Gladstone objected that Britain was not 'the new Rome' and had no special 'imperial mission'. What Disraeli meant, Gladstone argued in his Third Midlothian speech, was simply this:

> Liberty for ourselves, Empire over the rest of mankind ... the policy of denying to others the rights that we claim ourselves. ... No doubt, gentlemen, Rome may have had its work to do, and Rome did its work. But modern times have brought a different state of things. Modern times have established a sisterhood of nations, equal, independent; each of them built up under that legitimate defence which public law affords to every nation, living within its own borders, and seeking to perform its own affairs.[10]

Yet, in Gladstone's formulation, these principles were not supposed to have universal application. On the whole they were limited, first, to 'the Christian nations of the world', and, second, to non-Christian nations with a stable government or ruler with whom Britain could establish treaties and formal agreements: the Ottoman Empire, China or Japan, and the Emir of Afghanistan or the Zulu king (see below, pp. 87–8). Moreover, though his dislike for imperialism was genuine, there was no hint of pacifism in his principles, but only a resolute attempt to promote peace, and regulate and restrain the use of force by subjecting it to international authority.

That this set of qualifications could have important implications was seen after his return to power in April 1880. At first the Concert of Europe was effectively revived and turned its attention to the Ottoman Empire, which was prevailed upon to cede the Adriatic port of Dulcigno to Montenegro. Soon, however, Gladstone's Liberal government became involved in a series of colonial wars. In terms of their cost to the British (and Indian) taxpayer, these conflicts – including the first Boer War in 1881, the invasion of Egypt in 1882 and the Sudan campaign of 1884–85 – far exceeded any of Beaconsfield's 'misdeeds'. In terms of international relations the result was even more disastrous: both the credibility of the Liberal government and the very existence of a 'Concert' of Europe were undermined. Britain and France found themselves at loggerheads, while Russia resumed its expansion in Afghanistan and most European countries embarked on the 'scramble for Africa'.

However, it is doubtful whether the British government could have done anything to prevent such developments. Part of the problem was that the network of international relations had changed considerably since 1871: German unification and the humiliation of France had profoundly altered the balance of power in Europe. Gladstone's difficulties were compounded by the new European eagerness to establish or enlarge colonial empires which, from the early 1880s, had begun to affect both the new powers (Germany and Italy) and the French Republic: all *argued* in terms of 'commercial interests', but in fact, in most cases, the new colonial empires were expressions of frustrated nationalism and an attempt to demonstrate national prowess on the cheap.

The British position was not made any easier by the fact that between Bismarck and Gladstone there was little love lost: while the two had more in common than either cared to admit, Bismarck disliked Gladstone as the international symbol of a constitutional system alternative to the one he had founded in the *Kaiserreich*. Prussian and German Liberals looked up to the G.O.M., and dreamt of replacing the Iron Chancellor in Germany with a 'Gladstone government', by which they meant a Liberal government with a strong parliamentary leader. The fact that their policy was supported by the Crown Prince Frederick and his wife, Victoria (daughter of the British queen), further increased

Bismarck's antipathy to Gladstone. Furthermore, the two statesmen had different visions of international relations. Gladstone still pursued the restoration of the 'Concert of Europe', based on the balance of power and joint action between the 'Big Five' (Britain, France, Germany, Austria-Hungary and Russia). Bismarck used the 'Concert' and kept it alive, as seen at the Berlin Congresses of 1878 and 1884–85.[11] However, in practice, he relied on controlled tension between the powers, taking care to play one against another (and particularly France against Britain), in order to avoid the danger of German isolation.

Nevertheless, Bismarck's approach offered no long-term solutions and did much 'to perpetuate the sense of irrevocable antagonisms which after a certain point seemed to paralyse all capacity for constructive negotiation'.[12] By contrast, and despite its failure in the short term, 'the essential Gladstonian plan of the collective guarantee of the common interests' was to be revived by the League of Nations after the First World War, and, with greater success, by various organizations after 1945. Moreover, Gladstone's ideas, including his desire to expose diplomacy to popular scrutiny, were to exercise great influence on both British and American Liberals and Progressives, including President Woodrow Wilson and many in the Labour and pacifist movements from the late nineteenth century onwards.

Gladstone and Britain's Imperial Role

Gladstone's fame as an imperial reformer is based on his life-long preference for self-government rather than direct rule, and for conciliation rather than repression. He insisted that the Empire was essentially a community of countries held together by loyalty to British culture and by shared economic interests in a free-trade world. He had developed this 'proto-Commonwealth' vision from Edmund Burke – particularly from the latter's analysis of the 1776 crisis in the Thirteen Colonies, and his stipulation that imperial rule could be founded only on an equitable reconciliation of British interests with those of the natives.

As Gladstone declared in a speech in 1853, this could best be achieved through the extension of self-government and 'the principle of local freedom'. For various reasons, including contemporary racial prejudice and the constraints inherent in a policy of imperial security (to which *all* British governments – irrespective of their political inclination – were obviously committed), such a policy was easier to implement in the colonies of 'white' settlement than, let us say, in India. Yet, even with regard to India and Africa Gladstone emerged as a consistent advocate of limited 'local freedom'. Moreover, in the heyday of Victoria's rule, Gladstone stood out against the rising tide of militant jingoism, and advocated national restraint, proposing policies which some contemporaries hailed as God-inspired, though others deplored as a wholesale surrender of imperial pride and interests to the foreigner and the 'savage'.

These principles were tested during his second administration (1880–85). When Gladstone returned to power in the spring of 1880 at the head of a large Liberal majority, his priorities were to purge the country of 'the fit of delirious Jingoism' – allegedly provoked by the previous Conservative government – and to restore commercial prosperity and high levels of employment. These two aims were inextricably linked, as trade problems and the rise in unemployment were widely ascribed to the 'wars and rumours of wars' which had characterized the latter part of Disraeli's government, and particularly the years 1878–80. As we have already seen,[13] with typical energy Gladstone set out to pacify the Empire and restore the economy, but from the beginning of 1881 his government ran into major difficulties, as imperial commitments entangled the country in a number of new colonial and international crises – particularly in South Africa and Egypt.

In the case of South Africa, when the Boers took up arms against British rule, Gladstone was faced with the alternative of enforcing large-scale repression or conceding something like independence: he opted for the latter course, even at the cost of giving the impression that he was 'capitulating to the rebels'. This move from coercion to conciliation was the prelude to a similar change in Irish policy from 1886. In India, too, there followed an important move towards a more liberal regime with the appointment of Lord Ripon as Viceroy. The establishment of forms of representative government at the provincial level, the repeal of the restrictive Vernacular Press Act and the passing of the Ilbert Act, which gave Indian magistrates jurisdiction over Europeans, were highly controversial among the British community in India. Gladstone, however, firmly supported Ripon all the way along. This was the context in which the first Indian National Congress

(1883–85) was established as an organization basically inspired by the ideals of Gladstonian Liberalism.[14]

Rather different was the outcome of Liberal policy in Egypt. British involvement in the Suez Canal Company – together with Anglo-French financial control of the country and the imposition of a British-friendly Khedive – generated growing discontent and hastened the formation of a nationalist movement spearheaded by officers of the Egyptian army. Gladstone initially regarded this movement with sympathy, but in the course of 1882, local British officials, fiercely hostile to the nationalists, managed to convince him that the situation was degenerating into anarchy and military despotism. When a majority of Liberal ministers demanded the forcible restoration of the status quo, Gladstone was apparently reluctant to act. However, once embarked upon a policy of intervention, he pursued it without misgivings. Militarily successful, it soon emerged that the operation had opened a veritable Pandora's Box of troubles for the Liberal government. Like the Americans in many of their late twentieth-century semi-colonial involvements in Asia and Latin America, the British in Egypt found that their 'police' operation had to be prolonged indefinitely in order to fill the power and legitimacy vacuum created by their own intervention.

Contemporary critics and many modern historians have claimed that the Egyptian imbroglio revealed the full degree of duplicity and hypocrisy inherent in Gladstone's Liberalism, since his commitment to peace and international justice seemed to apply only when a Conservative government was in office. Such criticism is not completely unfair, though, on the whole, it is based on a series of misunderstandings. First we must remember that, as H. C. G. Matthew has pointed out,[15] Gladstone's notion of international justice was limited explicitly to the Christian world,[16] with the qualified addition of the Ottoman Empire. As for the rest – including Afghanistan and Zululand – he applied general humanitarian considerations, such as respect for human life and avoidance of any unnecessary bloodshed, but recognized no inalienable right to either self-determination or self-government for countries which, like Egypt, had long lost both their independence and, as he thought, their national identity. Second, we must also bear in mind that Gladstone was in no way hostile to empires, whose legitimacy he did not question. He simply insisted that within such realms – whether British, Austrian or Ottoman – respect for 'local freedom' should be the general guideline. Coupled with the principles of the

'Third Midlothian Speech' quoted above, such a vision could be mis-
taken for a blanket endorsement of national aspirations, although, as
D. Schreuder has pointed out, it was actually 'concerned . . . with both
liberal reform (devolution, autonomy, freedom, voluntaryism) and
imperial conservation (reserved powers, delineated responsibility, cir-
cumscribed status, and qualified home rule in colonial societies)'.[17]

Finally, it must be observed that, in contrast to radical pacifists like
John Bright, Gladstone accepted that coercion might sometimes be
necessary as a short-term restraint for 'evil' tendencies and 'irrational'
behaviour, which, as a Christian, he saw as being deeply rooted in fallen
human nature. Thus, Liberal imperial policy consisted in moving from
occasional and limited coercion back to appeasement as the general
rule. Given that conciliation was the aim and self-government the
method, coercion might be applied whenever the circumstances
required.

It has been suggested by some historians that there was a fundamental distinctiveness in the Liberal approach to imperial reform:
Gladstone's model 'for colonies of non-white settlement . . . whether
Jamaica or India, was the empire of Rome' rather than the 'Greek
model' of self-governing territories, reserved for the 'white settle-
ments'.[18] It is true that such a position was held explicitly by some
members of Gladstone's first and second governments, including
Joseph Chamberlain, who had strong misgivings about any further
extension of Indian self-government. However, as far as Gladstone is
concerned, it is difficult to see how such a sharp distinction can be
maintained. When we consider his preference for 'indirect rule' and
colonial assemblies based on limited electoral franchises in both India
and Egypt, as well as his concern that representation and financial
responsibility should go hand in hand, it is problematic to argue that
the aims and strategies of his policy in India, and indeed in Egypt or
Jamaica,[19] were fundamentally different to those he employed in the
British Isles.

Gladstone was aware of the tension between what he described as the
'Christian races' and the 'Muslim races', but to him the differences
which mattered were cultural, not biological. Overseas he had little
interest in either establishing or preserving British control over peoples
of darker pigmentation in tropical regions: he was much more concerned to identify those social groups which – whether native or European – could become Britain's local economic partners and political
allies. Empire was, from this point of view, a means to an end: and the

end was the creation and expansion of a political and economic system based on those 'bourgeois' values which he perceived as foundational both for modernization and social development in a capitalist, free-trade world economy.

6

IRELAND

Containing Nationalism: 1880–1885

In his first attempt to 'pacify Ireland' (1869–73; see Chapter 3) Gladstone's thinking had followed a classical Whig blueprint:[1] his aim was to achieve religious and social integration at the expense of the established Episcopal Church of Ireland. Even his ill-fated effort to improve Irish university education was not particularly innovative, and followed the Peelite and Whig strategy of trying to 'neutralize' the state in its dealings with various religious bodies, while encouraging cross-community integration in the training of a new professional middle class. This strategy was based on the assumption that at the root of the Irish Question there was a need for social justice and greater civil liberty, rather than a demand for national independence. In the mid-nineteenth century such a view had been widely shared by both British and European observers, including J. S. Mill, Tocqueville, Cavour and Mazzini.[2] Even after 1868, and despite episodes of Fenian violence, there was little indication of a 'national' question in Ireland: there was no Home Rule party in Parliament – where the Irish MPs sat as either Liberal or Tory – and no nationalist movement in the country. After all, Fenianism was mainly an imported movement which lacked mass support in the country.

By 1873 English observers might have thought that the reforms implemented by the Liberal government, however incomplete, would be sufficient to stabilize the situation. However, with the onset of the agricultural depression, the extent to which Ireland had *not* been 'pacified' became evident. The escalating number of evictions and related 'outrages' (as ejected tenants fought back to retain control of the land) provided the background for the rise of the Irish Land

League and the Home Rule party. Originally established under Isaac Butt between 1870 and 1873, under the leadership of Charles Stewart Parnell from 1879, the Home Rule or National party adopted a platform which combined constitutional with social reform: it demanded both the restoration of the ancient Dublin Parliament and 'tenant right' for the farmers. Benefiting from the new conditions created by franchise reform and the 1872 Ballot Act, in 1874 it achieved considerable electoral success, chiefly at the expense of Gladstone's party: whereas in 1868 the Liberals had won 66 out of the 115 Irish seats, in 1874 they were almost replaced by the Home Rulers, who gained 60 seats, two of which were in Ulster. The following years confirmed the change in the political climate. While the agricultural situation did not improve under the 1874–80 Conservative government, the political balance among the Irish parties showed further consolidation by the Home Rulers under the leadership first of Isaac Butt, and, later, of Charles Stewart Parnell.

Thus, by the time Gladstone emerged from his semi-retirement in 1876–79, it was plain that something drastic had to be done in order to stem the tide of rural unrest and political nationalism. In 1877, when he visited Ireland to receive the freedom of the city of Dublin, Gladstone indicated his willingness to resume reform, singling out land and local government as the two areas which demanded immediate attention. The opportunity for a fresh approach to the Irish problem came in 1880, when Gladstone again became Prime Minister. Despite the fact that he was leading a large Liberal majority, comparable in size to the one of 1868, there was now a significant change in the balance of forces in Parliament: while in the past a considerable proportion of the Liberal majority had been Irish, in 1880 Liberals were clearly an endangered species in Ireland, regardless of their temporary revival in Ulster. Their cross-community stance, secular outlook on educational matters and focus on moderate social and economic reform cut little ice with the increasingly polarized Irish electorate, where allegiances and policies were determined by religious and ethnic background.

If we consider both Gladstone's second and third governments as a unit, three phases can be distinguished in his Irish strategy during the years 1880–86: first, additional, radical, land reform (1881); then, full equality of political and electoral rights between Ireland and Britain (1883–85); finally, legislative autonomy with a Parliament in Dublin subordinated to the 'Imperial Parliament' at Westminster (1886–94), accompanied (in 1886) by a proposal for further land reform.

In 1880–81 land reform could be pursued in two different ways. One option was to strengthen the 1870 Act: this implied 'tenant right' and the adoption of 'The Three F's' – fixity of tenure, fair rent and freedom of sale – as requested by the Land League, the militant organization of Irish tenant farmers. The other option was that of buying off the Anglo-Irish landlords at public expense, by means of a Treasury advance repayable by terminable annuities. This would enable the tenants to purchase the farms on which they worked, but would involve complex financial and political arrangements. Furthermore, Gladstone preferred, if possible, to preserve the Anglo-Irish gentry in their role of economic elite, something which could only be achieved if they retained ultimate control of the land.[3] Significantly, here he agreed with Charles Stewart Parnell.[4]

For all these reasons, in 1881 some watered-down version of 'tenant right' was Gladstone's preferred approach. Though the 1881 Land Bill offered less than the Land League demanded, in social terms it was still a radical proposal: it implied the establishment of a sort of condominium between landlords and tenants, in the sense that the latter would share some of the rights commonly associated with property. Thus occupancy would involve 'free sale' – the right to 'sell' their tenure to an incoming tenant of their own choice. Moreover, until they decided to leave, they would enjoy 'fixity', or full security against eviction (the only ground for which would be the non-payment of rent). Finally, the rent they were expected to pay would not be regulated by the law of supply and demand and other market considerations, but by social concerns. This was the third 'F': rents ought to be 'fair', that is, commensurate with the tenant's ability to pay. Special Land Courts would be appointed to ensure that they would be adjusted whenever and wherever they were found to be excessive.

This judicial imposition of socially acceptable rents was perhaps the Bill's most radical feature, and sanctioned an unprecedented degree of state intervention in the labour market. Many English and Scottish landlords were horrified, and some, like the Duke of Argyll, found the Bill so unacceptable that they resigned from the Liberal party. It was the beginning of a trend which would soon deprive Gladstone of most of his support among the landed aristrocracy.

Despite the apprehension generated by the Bill among the British gentry, Gladstone regarded Irish land reform as a special case, which would provide no precedent for equivalent change in the rest of the United Kingdom. In particular, he did not envisage an extension of tenant right to England. When eventually, in 1886, his third government introduced a similar Land Bill for the Scottish crofters in the Highlands, Gladstone saw this measure, too, as exceptional: the Highlands and Ireland shared not only special economic problems but also unusual social tensions. Furthermore, both possessed a Celtic culture, with its typical communal approach to land tenure, which, it was argued, was hardly compatible with Anglo-Norman assumptions about private property. Notions of the unusual nature of these two cases had been developed by both historians and philologists throughout the second half of the nineteenth century. Influenced by German historicism and historical linguistics,[5] English and Scottish scholars had begun to question old Utilitarian assumptions about the uniformity of human nature and of 'rational' legislation. Their conclusion was that each country and culture had its own peculiar history and context, and that it was within such a framework that reforms needed to be conceived. Incidentally, this also was the approach increasingly adopted by the Colonial and India Offices in their dealings with British dependencies in Asia and Africa, especially as far as land tenure was concerned.

Simultaneously, in order to curb the agrarian terrorism of the Land League, Gladstone introduced a Coercion Bill. This combination of concession and repression had the desired effect. On the one hand, coercion held down the Land League, whose leaders (including Parnell) were either imprisoned or forced to emigrate; on the other, concession undermined the motivation of the rank and file. When the farmers found that the law was of more advantage to them than revolution, they began crowding the newly established Land Courts, rather than supporting the League. By December 1881 the land agitation was decimated and Parnell was ready to cooperate with the government. The change was ratified by the so-called 'Kilmainham treaty', when Parnell was released from prison in exchange for his promise of support for law and order, while the Arrears Act extended the operation of the Land Act to the tenants who had contracted debts.

Thus, one of the long-term effects of this blending of reform and repression was to turn a semi-revolutionary situation in Ireland into one in which grievances were voiced through legal and political channels. By showing that violence was counterproductive, and that the law provided more effective instruments for protest, Gladstone laid the ground for a rebirth of Irish constitutional nationalism. In a sense he was transplanting 'popular liberalism' to Ireland.

From the point of view of the British Liberal party the problem was
that this new Irish 'popular liberalism' was nationalist, and regarded
Home Rule as its supreme aim. It was difficult to cooperate with it
without accepting its programme, at least in part. On the other hand,
contemplation of further concessions by the government was made
difficult by continuing episodes of violence which reached a climax in
May 1882, when agents of a nationalist splinter group murdered the
newly appointed Irish Secretary in Phoenix Park. He was Lord Frederick Cavendish, the husband of one of Gladstone's nieces and brother
of Lord Hartington. The Prime Minister had been very close to him,
and his death was a major blow to Gladstone personally, as well as to
Hartington, and, in political terms, to the cause of Irish constitutional
nationalism. Parnell himself was so shocked that he offered to resign.
Though eventually he continued as leader of the National party, a
renewal of coercion was under these circumstances inevitable.

However, no one, not even the Conservatives, regarded repression
as a feasible long-term solution. Rural unrest needed to be tackled by
addressing and removing its causes. The question was raised indirectly
even by the Conservatives, who, after the 1881 Land Act, began to
consider that buying off the Anglo-Irish aristocracy would be prefer-
able to a continuation of the new condominium. As the trade crisis
deepened under the effects of the spiralling decline in agricultural
prices, and outrages continued, Gladstone himself began to contemplate this particular solution. However, to him the wide-ranging financial operation involved in establishing a class of independent farmers
could not be carried out without first establishing local representative
authorities. By organizing and collecting the reinbursement of the loan
which the Treasury would provide, and by creating an indigenous
focus for complaints, such authorities could mediate political and social
tensions between the British Treasury and Irish farmers, and thus
guarantee political stability and a responsible management of the financial operation.

The Democratic Experiment: 1883–1885

However, the next step in Gladstone's attempt to 'pacify Ireland' consisted in the electoral reforms of 1883–85. These were part of a broader
and more ambitious plan to rationalize the entire representative system

of the United Kingdom. As Gladstone wrote to Lord Granville early in 1883, '[t]wo subjects, which have all along been contemplated as belonging to the mission of the present Parliament, are (1) Local Government in Great Britain [and Ireland] together with financial changes appertaining to it, and (2) the Representation of the People, in which latter I include Franchise and Redistribution'.[6] While the introduction of local government was postponed, for reasons which will be discussed in the next section, franchise reform was indeed implemented, and preceded by a draconian Act to curb bribery and corruption at elections (1883), and followed by the redistribution of seats (1885). The latter redesigned parliamentary boundaries across the United Kingdom on the basis of small, single-member constituencies (though some two-member constituencies survived), abolished the old county/borough division, and reduced the discrepancy in proportion between large and small constituencies. Together, these three electoral reforms brought about the greatest restructuring of the British representative system in the nineteenth century.

It is interesting that, despite heavy demands on his time and energy due to a series of imperial crises (see Chapter 5), Gladstone devoted much care and attention to the details of electoral reform, and ensured its difficult passage through Parliament. This involved a protracted struggle with the House of Lords, which, under Lord Salisbury, was effectively trying to prevent the passing of the franchise Bill unless it was accompanied by redistribution, which the Conservatives hoped to shape in the way best suited to their party interests. In response the Prime Minister conducted a vigorous campaign of public speeches around the country en route to his Midlothian constituency. In the end, however, a compromise was reached and redistribution passed in 1885 as a bipartisan measure.

The Tories were not the only obstacle to reform: the preparation of the relevant Bills involved Gladstone in a huge diplomatic effort to persuade recalcitrant Whigs – including some of his leading front-benchers – to come to terms with what they saw as another 'leap in the dark' of popular politics. In particular, Gladstone conducted a vast correspondence with Lord Hartington and Lord Spencer, both of whom resisted reform, but for different reasons. Hartington feared for the preservation of aristocratic influence in the counties. Spencer, the Viceroy of Ireland, feared that the extension of the county franchise to that turbulent isle would enfranchise more rebellious tenant farmers, thus bolstering both Parnell's nationalism and further demands for land reform. Though some historians have suggested that the Whigs retained a considerable dynamism and could have provided alternative leadership for the Liberal party had Gladstone 'vanished' from the political scene,[7] the 1884 reform crisis confirmed that they were already moving towards the right. Had Gladstone retired in 1885, as he had planned, it is difficult to see how the Whigs could have found either the political will or the ideological flexibility to lead the Liberal party, whose new electors demanded policies which the landed aristocracy found increasingly unpalatable.

The Third Reform Act established a uniform household franchise with a residence qualification throughout the United Kingdom, for both boroughs and counties. Though it was no substitute for universal suffrage, which some radicals continued to demand, its democratic impact should not be underestimated. As a system it was socially inclusive and effectively representative. Though only about 65 per cent of the adult male population was enfranchised at any given time between 1885 and 1918 (people were periodically disenfranchised, for example, through changes of residence), exclusion from the franchise was not based on criteria of either social status or ethnicity. Rather, the system tended to discriminate against the younger males, irrespective of class or regional background. This happened because, in order to qualify as householders, men had to be registered as resident ratepayers. Residence with one's parents did not count, though a few better-off men could claim the franchise on the basis of the very restrictive and arbitrary £10 'lodger' franchise. On the whole, however, especially in the counties, the proportion of working men on the registers varied with the proportion of the working class within the population as a whole. Insofar as there was a bias towards the middle classes, it was statistically marginal. Thus the 1884 Act created something like a 'democracy' of husbands (and, to a lesser extent, elder brothers), one which cut across both class and ethnic lines. These mature men – who held most positions of power and authority both at the workplace and within the power structure of the Victorian family – were charged with the 'virtual representation' of dependent younger males, as well as of their womenfolk. Such overlap between franchise and social structure helps to explain why household democracy turned out to enjoy a considerable level of legitimacy, and became the lasting boundary of the 'Pale of the Constitution'. Often challenged, but never reformed, it was to provide the framework for late Victorian and Edwardian politics until 1918.

Part of the popularity of the new system derived from the fact that it established uniform criteria of electoral representation throughout the United Kingdom, including Ireland, which in the past had been under special arrangements and franchises. If one considers the problems created by Parnell and the Land League for the Government in 1880–84, it is difficult to escape the conclusion that the extension of the household county franchise in Ireland was a gamble, rather than a courageous reform. However, the Prime Minister was of the opinion that no reform Bill which excluded Ireland would be acceptable to Parliament. Moreover, in order to defuse the nationalist time bomb, the Liberal leader was trying to convince the Irish that the Union could be made to 'work' for them.

We may wonder why Gladstone did not consider more carefully the option of proportional representation, supported by Lord Hartington and others: arguably, its application would have helped to moderate nationalism and regional allegiances within a society which was undergoing a process of fragmentation. However, proportional representation, with its emphasis on 'personal' rather than 'community' representation, was in contrast to the British tradition of territorial constituencies; furthermore, however helpful in Ireland, it did not seem to be relevant to the rest of the United Kingdom.

Home Rule: 1881–1894

When Beaconsfield, in his 1880 electoral 'manifesto', warned that the Liberals were moving towards the adoption of Home Rule for Ireland, Gladstone responded in carefully measured words, telling his electors that

> an attempt is made to work upon your fears by dark allusions to the repeal of the union and the abandonment of the colonies. Gentlemen, those who endangered the union with Ireland were the party that maintained there an alien church, an unjust land law, and franchises inferior to our own; and the true supporters of the union are those who firmly uphold the supreme authority of parliament, but exercise that authority to bind the three nations by the indissoluble tie of liberal and equal laws.[8]

Obviously, Beaconsfield was not totally wrong, except in the timing. On the other hand, neither in 1880 nor in 1886 did Gladstone see Home Rule – or any other form of Irish self-government – as tantamount to the 'repeal of the Union'. His general attitude to the question was shaped by two factors: his dislike for the administrative centralization typical of the British Parliamentary system, and his debt to Edmund Burke.

As far as the first is concerned, from at least 1872 Gladstone had considered wide-ranging reform plans for the whole system of local government. His ideas acquired special significance in the Irish context after 1874, in view of the rise of the Home Rule party. Thus, in 1877 during his visit to Dublin, Gladstone deplored centralization and extolled the virtues of local self-government. Later, in a letter to Lord Granville, he commented:

> Had the Home Rulers a real leader whom they were disposed to follow I cannot think it would be difficult to arrange a *modus vivendi* with them. As to any thing more than that I am not sanguine, even if I suppose my own opinions about Local Government to be those of the party, which they are not, for I go much farther than the 'average' Liberal.[9]

Between 1881 and 1885 Gladstone acted upon his word as far as land and electoral reforms were concerned. When his original plan did not result in political 'pacification', partly because only peasant proprietorship would satisfy the land agitation, Gladstone began to pursue the 'binding of the three nations' by different means. If further land reform was necessary, and if it required the reform of local government, then the latter was to be considered a priority. Indeed, as early as 1882 he wrote to Forster, the Irish Secretary:

> About Local Government for Ireland... Until we have seriously responsible bodies to deal with us in Ireland, every plan we frame comes to Irishmen, say what we may, as an English plan. As such it is probably condemned. At best it is a one-sided bargain, which binds us, not them.... If we say we must postpone the question till the state of the country is more fit for it, I should answer that the least danger is in going forward at once. It is liberty alone, which fits men for liberty.... for the Ireland of today the first question is the rectification of the relations between the landlord

and tenant, which is happily going on; the next is to relieve Great Britain from the enormous weight of the Government of Ireland unaided by the people, & from the hopeless contradiction in which we stand while we give a Parliamentary representation hardly effective for anything but mischief, without the local institutions of self-government which it presupposes, & on which alone it can have a sound and healthy basis.[10]

One of the obstacles in the way of proceeding with the extension of Irish self-government was Lord Hartington's strong opposition, which he voiced publicly in a speech in January 1883. Though Gladstone was still far from endorsing Home Rule, this was an early warning of 'the radical difference of opinion' (Gladstone's own words) which was eventually to split the party in 1886. While the Prime Minister reiterated his strong commitment to 'decentralising doctrines', he commented privately that '[t]he argument that we cannot yet trust Irishmen with popular local institutions is the mischievous argument by which the Conservative opposition to the Melbourne Government resisted, and finally crippled, the reform of municipal corporation in Ireland'.[11] In February 1883 Gladstone referred explicitly to the desirability of reorganizing the United Kingdom in such a way as to separate the administration of Irish affairs from those of the rest of the country, provided the supremacy of 'the Imperial Parliament' was safeguarded. In the context of his well-known support for self-government and his Burkean theory of 'local freedom' for the colonies, this was a somewhat explicit statement of policy intent. In Ireland as much as in the colonies, self-government was the key to political stability and efficient administration:

Under the present highly centralised system of Government, every demand, which can be started on behalf of a poor and ill-organised country, comes directly to the British Government and Treasury; if refused it becomes at once a head of grievance, if granted not only a new drain but a certain source of political complication and embarassment, the peasant proprietary – the winter's distress – the state of the labourers – the loans to farmers – the promotion of public works – the encouragement of fisheries – the promotion of emigration – each and every one of these questions has a sting, and the sting can only be taken out of it by our treating it in correspondence with a popular and

responsible *Irish* body – competent to act for its own portion of
the country.[12]

During these years various proposals were examined, including the
Provincial Councils Bill in 1882, and, in 1885, both Childers's plan for
'federal home rule' and the Chamberlain–Dilke proposition for the
establishment of county councils under a Dublin 'Central Board',
which would control the Irish executive. The main stumbling block
was, again, the existence of strong differences within the government,
now polarizing around the younger Whigs (Hartington and Harcourt),
on the one hand, and the younger Radicals (Chamberlain and Dilke) on
the other. In May 1885, in the memorandum of a conversation with
Granville about the Central Board proposal, Gladstone wrote:

Under the circ[umstance]s . . . the present aspect of affairs was of a
probable split, *independently* of the question what course I might
individually pursue.
My opinions I said were very strong and inveterate. I did not
calculate upon Parnell and his friends, or upon Manning and his
Bishops. Nor was I under any obligation to follow or act with
Chamberlain. But independently of all questions of party, of
support & of success, I looked upon the extension of a strong
measure of Local Govt. like this to Ireland . . . as invaluable
itself. . . .[13]

However, nothing concrete came of these discussions at the time,
chiefly because – as we have seen – the government was defeated on
the 1885 budget, and resigned. At the ensuing general election, with
the exception of Ulster, Ireland voted for Parnell's National party,
which obtained large majorities in most constituencies. Such a poll
under the new and more representative electoral system was like a
national referendum for Home Rule. Before the election Gladstone
had feared that the nationalists would gain as many as eighty seats;
when they actually obtained eighty-five, plus one seat in Liverpool, he
relinquished his residual doubts about Parnell's right to speak for what
Gladstone regarded as a 'nation'.
    The time had come for a further experiment in Burkean reform,
one which he had been mulling over for several years. For, in contrast
to what two scholars have argued in a controversial book,[14] there was
no 'sudden conversion', but only a gradual evolution of Gladstone's

thought on the question of Home Rule.[15] It was a slow process, which
gradually unfolded in the typically empirical–historicist way that Gladstone had derived from Bishop Butler and Edmund Burke. Gladstone's admiration for the great Anglo-Irish philosopher had not
weakened over the years since he left the Conservative party. During
his second and third governments his diaries contain entries which
eloquently illustrate the extent to which he continued to be under
Burke's spell.[16] He searched Burke's writings for inspiration and 'analogies' especially in times of crisis. Thus, in 1886 he wrote to the editor
of *The Spectator* arguing the case for Home Rule in the following terms:

> For opponents I generally have four prescriptions. 1. Study the
> abominable, the almost incredible history of the Union. . . 2. Soak
> & drench yourselves with the writings of Mr. Burke on Ire-
> land...most of all with his writings on the American War. 3.
> Look a little at the effects of Home Rule (a) in Europe (b) in the
> colonies...4. Consider a little what is representation & what does
> it mean.[17]

The implications are not difficult to see: statesmen should learn from
history as well as from their own personal experience, paying attention
to analogies and precedents drawn from both Europe and the colonies.
In this context they should consider the importance of representation
for the resolution of ethnic and regional conflicts and the preservation
of imperial unity; and, more generally, they should 'soak & drench
[themselves] with the writings of Edmund Burke'. Implicit in this
approach was a vision of what the British Empire ought to be. In
particular, 'Home Rule' in all its regional incarnations was an attempt
to implement such 'prescriptions' and legislate in such a way as to
provide a constitutional framework for peaceful and orderly progress.
The 'error' of 1776, which Britain ought to avoid in 1886, was that of
trying 'to hold the colonies by the mere exercise of power'.[18] Though
Ireland was not a colony in the constitutional sense of the expression,
the parallels – especially with the Thirteen Colonies – were quite
evident.

Gladstone believed that in choosing the way in which Ireland should
be governed, politicians ought to bear in mind the opinions of the local
population. His main mistake was that of not realizing the importance
of Protestant Ulster, or the extent of its opposition to Home Rule. Over
the next forty years the division within Ulster became a major stum-

bling block for both the Liberals and the Irish National party, reaching a climax in the agitation led by Sir Edward Carson in 1912–14. Yet, despite Protestant opposition, in 1886 Gladstone's strategy might have worked in Ulster as well as in the rest of the island, had Parliament approved the Home Rule Bill. After all, as in the rest of the British Isles, in the 1880s Ulster politics was still influenced by 'deference' to notables and respect for the authorities. There were neither armed volunteers in the Province, nor any mass agitation exploiting religious fears. If implemented, Home Rule might have generated riots, but the government would have had no difficulty in containing any disturbances through those moderate measures of coercion which Dublin Castle and the Royal Irish Constabulary were so accustomed to carry out in other parts of the isle.

While Gladstone did not fear Ulster, by the end of 1885 he had identified Parnell with a concrete and 'viable' solution similar to the one that he himself was considering and developing: indeed, as Colin Matthew has recently pointed out,[19] the Prime Minister drafted his Home Rule Bill two weeks after reading a paper by Parnell on the constitution of Ireland. Gladstone's model was the Canadian constitution of 1867,[20] rather than the contemporary continental European experiments of 'dual monarchies' (Sweden–Norway and Austria–Hungary). Though based upon the 1867 British North America Act, the 1886 Government of Ireland Bill ensured that the powers of the new Dublin Parliament would be more limited than those of its Canadian counterpart. Gladstone intended that the imperial government retain full control of defence, foreign affairs and trade policy. The latter was a sensitive question. One of the main concerns – both among the British public and the Ulster industrialists – was that the new Dublin government would abandon free trade and opt for protectionism, which would benefit only the farmers. Gladstone addressed this concern by making sure that under Home Rule Ireland would remain strictly linked to the rest of the United Kingdom not only politically, but also commercially.

The Irish Parliament would consist of two 'orders': the first would include elected MPs who would be returned – under the UK system of household franchise – for the constituencies created by the 1885 Redistribution Act. The second order would comprise both the Irish hereditary peers and a number of elected senators. The latter would be men of property and standing, and would be returned by a restricted electorate on a £25 franchise. The two orders would sit and deliberate together; however, each would have the power of veto, which could be exercised by voting separately whenever either so desired. Like Canada, Ireland after Home Rule would no longer be represented at Westminster. This feature had the advantage of cutting down the tasks of the overworked imperial Parliament, but alarmed Liberal imperialists, who saw it as a step towards full independence.

There is no doubt that Gladstone did not want independence for Ireland any more than he did for India.[21] His strategy was Burkean as to both ends and means. His aim was to make the Empire more flexible, less vulnerable to nationalist movements and easier to run by the traditional elites (which, in Ireland, were well represented by Parnell himself). Always hostile to metropolitian centralism, Gladstone insisted that the United Kingdom should experiment with the strategy already implemented by London in most of the 'white' colonies: representative decentralization. Its success in Canada – a society which, like Ireland, was divided not only between Protestants and Catholics but also between two distinct language groups with opposed national histories – encouraged a similar experiment in Dublin. Nationalism would then be 'contained and domesticated' through constitutional pluralism and Parliamentary sovereignty; 'government by consent could be rooted in Ireland, and law in Ireland made integral to its social attitudes, as has happened in Scotland'.[22]

The parallel with Scotland, and indeed Wales, played an important role in Gladstone's vision for a new relationship between the 'British *nations*' (he used the plural), Ireland and the Empire:

> I hold that there is such a thing as local patriotism, which, in itself, is not bad, but good.... the Scotch nationality is as strong as it ever was, and should the occasion arise... it will be as ready to assert itself as in the days of Bannockburn.... The Irishman is more profoundly Irish [than the Scot is Scottish]; but it does not follow that, because his local patriotism is keen, he is incapable of Imperial patriotism.[23]

While recognizing and valuing historical forces and traditions, Gladstone wanted to make sure that the energy which they generated would be harnessed and applied – like steam power in a locomotive – with a view to propelling the carriage of the imperial state. In the case of Ireland, as much as in those of Egypt, South Africa and Afghanistan – Gladstone was looking first and foremost for authoritative and representative mediators, on whom the British government could rely in order to institutionalize and resolve conflicts of interest. He preferred a stable interlocutor – even an independent or hostile one – to someone friendly to the British government, but who was unstable and non-representative. In 1881 Gladstone had seen Parnell as a demagogue prone to violence and despotism, and devoid of real national support (more or less as he saw Arabi Pasha in 1882). However, later developments, including the constitutional course adopted by the National party after the Land Act, had shown that he could be responsible and responsive. In 1885 he emerged as the chosen leader of five-sixths of the Irish people. The 1885 electoral results came to play a crucial role in Gladstone's rhetoric: the polls showed that '[a]t every stage, as the obstructions to national utterances [were] removed', '[a]s the popular representation [became] a reality', the Irish people confirmed their dislike for London rule, however well-meaning. Furthermore it confirmed

> [t]hat a people is the best judge of its own internal wants; that the Irish for this purpose are a people; that whatever power is added to the national stock by improved education, by extended franchises, or by even the humbler forms of local government, will all run into the one channel of steady, undying demand for the restoration of the national life by reviving, in Ireland's ancient capital, the management of Irish affairs. Some may even hold it to be most happy that the demand, as it has become sonorous, has also become...both determinate and safe.[24]

The ends Gladstone pursued in 1885–86 were not substantially different from those he had pursued in 1869–70: his ultimate aim was to make Ireland more similar to England,[25] a strategy not unlike his attitude to imperial dependencies, as discussed in Chapter 5. In 1886, as in 1869, Gladstone sought to 'pacify' Ireland and create a political and social system which would allow orderly economic progress and make coercion superfluous. He tried to establish a system which would require no further external intervention and which could be operated by the Irish, for their own benefit, within the British Empire. This new strategy had an important additional advantage: while repressing rebellious tenants was an expensive and distasteful business, liberty for the Irish would be accompanied by cheaper government for the Empire.

Yet, given the fact that one of Gladstone's aims was retrenchment, we may wonder why the Home Rule Bill was accompanied by a Land Purchase Bill which, as we shall see, proposed an unprecedented outlay of public expenditure for peace purposes. The answer is that by 1886 Gladstone had come to see the Irish Question as an imperial crisis on the scale of those faced by him in Egypt in 1882 and Afghanistan in 1885: the legislative proposals of 1886 were conceived as an attempt to prevent Irish secession by creating a stable social and constitutional system. Gladstone disliked land purchase, which he had tried to avoid with his 1881 legislation. But in 1885 the Conservatives passed the Ashbourne Act, which indicated the extent to which land purchase was both acceptable to the main groups in Parliament, and in a sense, almost inevitable.[26] If it was, indeed, 'inevitable', Gladstone wanted it to be both sensational (in the tradition of his 'great Bills') and decisive: like the 1882 war in Egypt, Gladstonian land purchase involved a massive investment of capital in the hope to solve – once and for all – an imperial crisis.

The 1886 Land Bill had two aims: to enable the Anglo-Irish aristocracy to sell their land, if they so wished, and withdraw from their often uncomfortable position vis-à-vis a rebellious tenantry; and to enable the tenants to purchase the farms on which they worked and then repay the mortgage over a number of years. The operation would have required the financial guarantee of the British Treasury, while the newly established Home Rule government would administer the repayment of the loans on the properties. The advantage of purchasing the land in one stroke, rather than by instalments (as the previous Conservative government had begun to do with the 1885 Ashbourne Act) was chiefly political: if adopted, the Land Purchase Bill would be a spectacular measure, whose social effect would be compounded by its psychological impact. On the one hand, a class of independent peasant farmers – alleged to be naturally conservative and respectful of law and property – would have been created in a comparatively short time. On the other, the Act would have portrayed the British government as generous and responsive to popular needs, once these were clearly expressed through a democratic and no longer corrupt representative system. Finally, the fact that Land Purchase would be accompanied by Home Rule meant that a responsible Irish government would have been charged with the management of the loans and their repayment, thus relieving London of the unpleasant duty of collecting rents from an Anglophobic and restless peasantry. The latter was crucial both in

Gladstone's view, and in the view of Sir Robert Hamilton, the Irish Viceroy's principal adviser. In a letter to Henry Fowler, in September 1884, Hamilton had pointed out that

> At the bottom of all real reform lies the introduction of a system of local government. This is a matter not alone of Irish but Imperial importance, and concessions made in the direction of spending more public money in Ireland as it is at present governed will only increase the difficulties of arranging matters hereafter. Short of separation, which is out of the question and which at present is only desired by a very small minority in Ireland, the fullest measure of self-government should be granted. If this is not done and done quickly we may have the bigger question of separation to combat. Under such local government mistakes would be made, but the people would be educated in self-dependence, and without this Ireland will be a constant and increasing source of trouble to successive administrations who will be attempting the impossible task of governing an educated people from outside instead of showing them and helping them to govern themselves.[27]

Thus, the Gladstonian line on both Home Rule and Land Purchase was that the two were inseparable. Self-government was fundamental to ensure a 'responsible' administration of the public funds whose outlay land reform would demand. In conclusion, only political responsibility could ensure financial rectitude and prevent land reform from sliding into 'reckless socialism', a tendency which, Gladstone thought, the Tories were cynically encouraging through piecemeal legislation like the Ashbourne Act.[28]

However, unfortunately for Gladstone, the Land Purchase Bill was perceived as unacceptably expensive by the majority of the British public, as well as by Parliament. It entailed, in Joseph Chamberlain's words, an 'enormous and unprecedented use of British credit'. Though Land Purchase was a feat of advanced social engineering, the Left disliked it. They strongly objected to the burdens it would impose on the British middle and working classes for the benefit of the despised Anglo-Irish landlords, who, the Radicals thought, were not entitled to any compensation at all. The exact cost of the operation was difficult to assess, given the voluntary nature of the scheme (landlords would not be forced to sell, only given the option to do so on reasonable terms).

However, the Treasury was expected to advance up to £120 million in five years (1886–90) at a borrowing rate of 3 per cent. In order to appreciate the scale of the proposal, we should bear in mind that this sum was the equivalent of 120 per cent of the 1885 budget, on which the previous Liberal government had been defeated.

As H. C. G. Matthew has convincingly argued,[29] from a financial point of view the Bill could easily have been implemented and would have been cheaper to operate than the Ashbourne Act, had the latter been used as the blueprint for such a comprehensive operation. It was, nevertheless, an extraordinary proposal, especially as Gladstone was now suggesting that a *social* problem should be solved by means of massive financial intervention by the Treasury.

Of course, in the long term the proposed measure was not particularly revolutionary: after all, the abolition of slavery in British colonies had been financed in a similar way in 1833. Moreover, state intervention in Ireland had no *necessary* implication for social policies in Britain. Nevertheless, Scottish landowners may have felt alarmed, in view of the fact that the land question in their country bore some resemblance to the problems in Ireland. Thus, two tantalizing questions arise: would Gladstone's historicist reformism have found its way into other parts of the United Kingdom, thus becoming, in practice, indistinguishable from the policies demanded by the most advanced radicals? How far had Gladstone moved away from laissez-faire? Writing towards the end of the 1920s, Herbert Gladstone argued that his father had never changed his basic assumptions in matters of finance and social policy:

> Individualism is the key to Mr Gladstone's action... through sixty years. By training and predilection he was at heart an individualist, *gradually yielding to demonstrated necessity of State action on a large scale* as he was driven to yield on a small scale even so early as 1843.... *Yielding at times to necessity,* he remained an individualist to the end.[30]

The phraseology in italics contains important qualifications: the choice between individualism and state intervention depended on the assessment of 'demonstrated necessities'. Whenever the evidence was found to be convincing, Gladstone was quite ready to move far beyond the ideas with which his name had been so long associated. His Anglican organicist vision of the state – deeply modified from 1832, but never fully rejected – was an additional variable in the complex equation of his attitudes to state intervention. Laissez-faire was thus qualified by an Evangelical/High-Church version of what German and Italian liberals called the 'ethical state': the notion that the state – though religiously neutral – had moral responsibilities to discharge.

Gladstone never became a convert to 'the New Liberalism', of which some of his junior colleagues – including Asquith and Lloyd George – were already spokesmen in the early 1890s. Indeed, it was only with great difficulty that he could be brought to accept the increased death duties introduced by Vernon Harcourt with the 1894 budget, when he was still Prime Minister. Yet it is important to remember that, while Gladstone had reluctantly endorsed the collectivist prescriptions of the 1891 Newcastle Programme of the National Liberal Federation,[31] he chose to resign on the issue of increased naval estimates. To him, military expenditure was still much less acceptable than expensive social reform, and both could be contemplated only in cases of demonstrated 'necessity'.

As is well known, both the Land Purchase and Home Rule Bills were effectively opposed by a coalition between Tories and dissident Liberals. The Liberal party split, with most of the Whigs (including Gladstone's heir apparent Lord Hartington) and some of the radicals (led by Chamberlain) voting with the Conservatives. The Liberal schism was further deepened at the following general election (June 1886), which resulted in a victory for the anti-Home Rule 'Unionist' coalition. The latter skilfully played the British nationalist card, though, arguably, it was the Liberals who were the true 'United Kingdom' party in 1886. On the one hand, the Conservatives voiced *English* nationalism, which was in increasingly strident contrast to the wishes and inclinations of the other component parts of the United Kingdom. On the other, the Liberal Unionists were a mixed band, which included old-fashioned libertarians who disliked Parnell's methods, Whigs who distrusted social radicalism, and radical imperialists who, fearing the disintegration of the state, compared the Home Rule with the secession crisis in the USA: they saw themselves opposing Parnell in the same spirit with which Abraham Lincoln had opposed Jefferson Davis in 1861–65. Simultaneously, many intellectuals moved away from Liberalism, under the impression that now Gladstone 'appealed to separatist sentiment in Scotland and Wales, as well as in Ireland. He appealed to the "masses" against the "classes". He appealed to ignorance against intelligence and the professions'.[32]

While the Conservatives, with Liberal Unionist support, went on to form a government (1886–92), Gladstone and his new Irish allies proceeded to reorganize their forces. By the late 1880s Parnell's MPs were joining the National Liberal Club: it seemed as if liberal constitutionalism was in the process of been fully transplanted to Ireland,[33] while Irish nationalism had become a reliable source of support for the Liberal party. By the end of the 1880s there were good prospects for a Liberal/Home Rule victory in the next general election.

However, in 1890 the famous Parnell divorce scandal split the Irish party and discredited the Gladstonian alliance. Yet, remarkably, the latter proved stronger even than Parnell's hitherto unchallenged personal appeal: when asked to choose between their leader and Gladstone, the Irish National party rejected Parnell and, by a margin of 43 to 27, chose to preserve the Liberal alliance. It was a vindication of Gladstone's strategy, but did not prevent the Irish party from losing support and credibility, amidst internecine strife, which continued even after Parnell's death in 1891. By the time the general election was called, in 1892, and despite a very energetic campaign, the Gladstonian–Nationalist coalition emerged with a majority of only forty over the Conservative–Unionist camp. This was sufficient to push a second Home Rule Bill through the Commons, though with the certainty that the House of Lords would reject it. When this happened Gladstone advised dissolution and a new general election on the issue of the Lords' constitutional powers. His colleagues, however, refused to support him, and Gladstone resigned and retired from public life in 1894. Despite his recommendation of Lord Spencer as his successor, the Queen chose Lord Rosebery, who subsequently led the party to a disastrous electoral defeat in 1895.

Home Rule and the Decline of the Liberal Party

By way of conclusion, it is appropriate to consider the impact of the Home Rule split on the performance of the Liberal party during the next thirty years. Some historians have seen 1886 as the 'crisis' of Liberalism, and have ascribed it to Gladstone's 'obsession' with Ireland,[34] which was, in their view, a mere sideshow, a pawn in the game between the two parties.[35] The extent to which this

interpretation ignores the political and constitutional reality of the
United Kingdom at the time is quite astonishing. It is important to
note that most of Gladstone's contemporaries took a different line:
indeed, the Irish issue generated an enormous amount of interest
and passion in Britain, and there is evidence to suggest that popular
support for Home Rule was culturally deeper, and politically much
more significant, than has hitherto been conceded.
   The traditional view is that British working-class voters were unin-
terested in Home Rule. Poll results seem to bear out this conclusion.
Yet, electoral evidence cuts both ways: after all, the Liberal party
retained most of its popular support both in 1886 and in 1892.
Furthermore, after Gladstone's retirement in 1894, his successors
remained loyal to Home Rule, which became one of the Liberal party's
trademarks.
   In terms of popular support it is also significant that from as early as
1874 most working-class parliamentary candidates and Lib-Lab MPs
endorsed the Irish demand for a Parliament in Dublin.[36] Behind such
support, the weight and significance of which would deserve a longer
discussion, there was an unbroken tradition of concern and sympathy
for what was described as 'the sister island'. The Chartists had consistently upheld the Irish demand for the repeal of the Act of Union, and
as late as the 1850s their last meetings had been enlivened by toasts 'to
the Irish patriots'. With the exception of parts of south-west Lancashire, where large-scale Irish immigration fuelled sectarian strife, it
would seem that post-Chartist agrarianism and radical hostility towards
the landed gentry were sufficient to counteract the traditional religious
animosity against the Catholics. Proposals for radical land reform and
even nationalization were commonplace in the radical press. In 1881
Gladstone's Land Act was welcomed as a major step in the right direc-
tion, but his renewal of coercion was taken as conclusive evidence that
the Home Rulers were right to demand constitutional reform and even
independence.[37] There was perplexity about a Liberal government
which had opposition MPs imprisoned and their peasant electors per-
secuted by armed police and prosecuted by special laws: such a policy
could not be continued for long without serious repercussions for the
party's credibility. By the end of 1885 the Irish crisis was providing the
anti-imperialist Left both with the opportunity to develop an alternative platform to the then official Liberal policy, and with the prospect of
mass support among working-class electors of Irish extraction. As
Henry Pelling has pointed out in one of his classical studies,[38] in the

heavy industrial areas of the north-east of England there was the distinct possibility that a combination of Joseph Cowen's money and leadership with Social Democratic ideas and personnel would soon lead to the formation of a powerful independent workers' party. Thus in 1885, as much as in 1899–1900 and 1916–22, the unity and viability of the Liberals as the workers' main party was threatened not by class struggle, but by 'external' questions such as Ireland, the Empire and foreign policy. By opting for Home Rule, Gladstone pre-empted a crisis on the left at the cost of another one on the right.

Furthermore Home Rule was not just an *Irish* question, but a *conglomerate* of questions, especially relevant to Scotland and Wales, where Gladstone succeeded in mobilizing the growing constituency of national revivalists. The papers of the Scottish Liberal Association (SLA) convey the idea of rank-and-file enthusiasm for Home Rule.[39] For the Liberal party's mass organization – which in Scotland was more influential than in England – Home Rule had two main attractions. First, as a bold measure of constitutional reform, it was associated with further steps towards democracy, including (from October 1887) the demand for 'one-man-one-vote', a shortening of the residential qualification and payment of MPs.[40] Second, Home Rule was also applicable to Scotland, where – as stated in a motion tabled by the Ayrshire Liberals – 'questions closely touching the welfare of the people, and long ripe for settlement, are from year to year superseded by the dominating influence of English interests and opinions in the Imperial Parliament'.[41] In other words, from 1887, in Scotland as in Ireland, Home Rule and social reform – which first and foremost meant land reform – were seen as two sides of the same coin. From 1889 Irish ideas began to influence SLA approaches to rural poverty in the Highlands, with demands that the government should 'relieve immediate wants of certain sections of the people, [by building] harbours, roads, railways, and other works of public utility'.[42] Thus, Ireland, far from being regarded as a 'special case', became a testing ground for the viability of new reform policies.

The Welsh Liberal response to Home Rule was equally enthusiastic, and fostered a strong indigenous nationalist movement which, as Lloyd George wrote to a correspondent, had completely 'captured' the Liberal organizations by 1895.[43] The latter's obsession with land reform and church disestablishment reflected nationalist concerns for which close Irish parallels could be indicated. The nearest of such parallels was perhaps the Tithe War of 1887, which like the Irish one of fifty-five years before, involved considerable violence, generated long-lasting bitterness and serious political effects, and indicated the extent of popular support for nationalism.

In focusing on Home Rule Gladstone provided his Scottish and Welsh supporters with an issue on which 'old' and 'new' Liberals could combine efforts. Cooperation was helped by the fact that both Liberal nationalism and the 'new' Liberalism were based on an organicist concept of society; both insisted on the link between civic virtue and social reform; and both used populist ideologies derived from some notion of class struggle, but ruled out a class-based political party system. Here it again becomes tempting to draw a parallel with Irish nationalism, one which was explicitly drawn at the time by the leading Welsh Liberal Tom Ellis. To Ellis the Irish question was 'so huge, fierce, volcanic,... so comprehensive that in fighting on its various issues we fight on principles which will have application far and outside Ireland, and not least in Wales'.[44] Like the Irish, Ellis saw Home Rule as 'a policy of prudence for labour... a policy of hope, of promise, of growth'.[45] For many Irish there was a close link between nationalism and religion. Ellis agreed: to him 'Welsh Nationalism [was] the political translation of the Methodist revival'.[46] An admirer of the Boer republics from as early as 1890, Ellis dreamed of a Wales of independent farmers. Significantly, his ideal of the masterless peasant-citizen was shared not only by contemporary Parnellite Nationalists, but especially by the rising generation of Sinn Fein activists, who would come to dominate Irish politics in the 1920s.[47]

Meanwhile, all over the United Kingdom class allegiances continued to be overridden by national and religious ones. As far as Ireland is concerned, this point has been clearly demonstrated by Claire Fitzpatrick in her study on Labour and Sinn Fein.[48] How comparable was the situation in Scotland and Wales? Before the First World War the parallels were more striking than the differences. For example, the electoral track record of the Scottish Labour party was dismal: as late as December 1910 it had only three MPs (in contrast to 58 Liberals and 9 Conservatives). One of the most important reasons for such a poor performance was summarized effectively by a disgruntled ILP candidate, John Robertson, in the aftermath of the socialist defeat in north-east Lanark in 1904: 'I need scarcely mention that the ministers and religious bodies of all denominations were against us.... Perhaps, after all, the strongest force against me in the fight was that... it was decided that the Irish vote should go Liberal...'.[49] The Presbyterian ministers and the Irish Land League (which had 100 branches in Scotland) had sealed his fate.

The most famous Lanarkshire socialist was of course, Keir Hardie, who was eventually returned by Merthyr, a Welsh two-member constituency, in 1900. There the senior member was D. A. Thomas, a wealthy pro-Boer Liberal, who wanted to be rid of his Liberal imperialist colleague, Pritchard Morgan. Thus, despite being a Labour candidate, Keir Hardie was elected with the sponsorship of a capitalist Liberal MP, and was successful not because he was a socialist, but because he was a pacifist, an Evangelical Nonconformist, a Celt (as he claimed), and a Welsh nationalist (as he affected).

In a justly influential piece of historical revisionism, Duncan Tanner has presented Liberalism and Labour in 1900–18 as two 'progressive' parties competing for the same social and political constituency. If Tanner's analysis is correct, we need to go a step further and recognize that in this competition the Liberals enjoyed an important advantage. Despite the electoral weakness of the party between 1895 and 1906, those who proposed left-wing alternatives to Liberalism discovered, to their cost, that they were competing against the combined forces of Christian radicalism and Celtic nationalism. When considered in a European context, this hold on both the Celtic and the Christian vote is a striking phenomenon; perhaps it was the single most important factor in postponing the rise of Labour until the 1920s.

EPILOGUE

[T]he English Government under [Gladstone's] guidance might be compared to the Athenian Government under the guidance of Pericles: 'it was nominally a democracy, but in reality the supremacy of the first citizen.'[1]

Issue No. 7755 of the *Economist* (April 1992) had a surprising cover illustration. It represented Gladstone wearing a flowery (perhaps 'postmodern') waistcoat and surrounded by the microphones of journalists, obviously eager to pick his brain on the current political situation. The title was – 'A prophet for the left'. The leading article presented the G.O.M. not as a historical figure, but as a model for both the modern Liberal Democrats and, especially, the Labour party. This was certainly remarkable, particularly after twelve years of Conservative governments, who had also claimed to be intent on restoring some of the traditional values and policies associated with Gladstonian liberalism. However, what is even more remarkable is that in 1997 a general election was won by a 'new' Labour party whose ideology seemed to have been expressly shaped along the lines suggested by *The Economist* five years earlier. Not only had Labour given up the socialist 'Clause IV' of its constitution, but the party's rhetoric and ideological outlook seemed much closer to those of traditional liberalism than to any recognizable form of socialism. Significantly, New Labour was on unusually good terms with the Liberal Democrats, and its manifesto was remarkable for a novel emphasis on constitutional, rather than social, reform. This included old liberal favourites, such as reform of both the electoral system and of the House of Lords (the focus of Gladstone's last parliamentary speech in 1894), and even Home Rule for both Wales and Scotland (which, as we have seen in Chapter 6, was first proposed by the Liberals in 1887). Not surprisingly, by 1998 comparisons between Blair and Gladstone had become commonplace, and indeed were encouraged by Tony Blair himself,[2] who seemed to regard Lord Jenkins of Hillhead – the Liberal Democrat peer and Gladstone's best-known biographer – as one of his 'mentors'.[3]

It is tempting to speculate on Gladstone's ultimate comeback in the shape of a Labour–Liberal coalition leading the country into the new millennium. Yet here the historian must exercise caution. Paraphrasing what Terry Jenkins has written in his *Disraeli*, also published in the present series, we must not forget that the historians' task is to present their complex subject 'free from the intellectual constraints imposed by . . . current partisan loyalties'.[4] Though many politicians – from Marco Minghetti in Risorgimento Italy to Tony Blair in EMU Britain – have derived inspiration from, or even tried to emulate, Gladstone, historians must insist that the G.O.M. be regarded as a unique historical character.

Gladstone was a Victorian shaped both by the strongly Evangelical culture of early nineteenth-century Britain, and by the formative experience of Peel's 1841–46 government. In some fundamental respects he remained a Peelite throughout his career, though from 1864 to 1868 he adopted an ambiguously democratic rhetoric in an attempt to modernize the Peel/Aberdeen government tradition and adapt it to the new realities of the extended franchise.

Then in 1876 the Bulgarian Agitation marked the beginning of a new phase in his career: during the last twenty years of his public life Gladstone's extra-parliamentary performances and charismatic public speaking became key features of his strategy to provide effective leadership for both the party and the nation. However, while Gladstone's style had changed, his aim remained that of converting 'the masses' to his version of the Peelite gospel.

Though contemporaries were often astonished by Gladstone's 'post-Bulgarian' boldness, his sophisticated populism was consistent with his religious outlook, his Evangelical background and his High Church proclivities. As a young man Gladstone had seriously considered becoming an ordained minister of the Church: it was fitting that, having become a statesman instead, he should import religious values and a revivalist style into the political realm. At the time revivalist religion represented the only experiment in mass communication which had been carried out successfully. The long-term growth of Victorian Nonconformity, and, from 1873–75, the impact of Moody and Sankey's dramatic evangelistic campaigns,[5] demonstrated that charismatic preaching provided an effective means of conveying *traditional* values and ideas to the masses. Gladstone – like his admirer and contemporary C. H. Spurgeon, the great Baptist preacher – tried to expound the old orthodoxy in a populist style: and, like Spurgeon, Gladstone was, to a large extent, successful.

In the *religious* sphere weekly Bible classes and chapel services helped to consolidate the conversions which had taken place during exhilarating 'monster meetings'. In the *political* sphere from 1877 the National Liberal Federation (NLF) became 'the covenanted church' of 'true believers', and helped to consolidate a particular form of Gladstonian orthodoxy. The NLF provided the bureaucratic back-up to stabilize 'conversions' and institutionalize the Liberal religion of the 'redeemed' masses – redeemed, that is, from the 'sins' of Tory jingoism and the pitfalls of the revamped socialist heresy.

Another way of looking at Gladstone in the context of his time is to compare him to the great American political orators of the pre-Civil War period, including Henry Clay (1777–1852), Daniel Webster (1782–1852) and John Calhoun (1782–1850). The leadership of these politicians sprang from social ascendancy, and their elaborate rhetoric reflected their aristocratic social status and education. Their success was possible partly because the United States in the 1840s, like Britain in the 1880s, combined a comparatively democratic franchise with residual popular 'deference' for traditional elites and their political style. Gladstone was fully conscious of the persistence of 'deference' politics in the democratized United Kingdom, and his overall strategy relied on the assumption that the landed aristocracy would be willing to continue to provide active leadership at both the local and the national level, not only in Britain but also in Ireland.[6] In this sense at least, Tollemache's comment on Gladstone's Periclean attitude to democracy – chosen as the opening quotation for this 'Epilogue' – was not unreasonable.

How, then, can we account for Gladstone's late Victorian reputation as a radical? It was due to a combination of three factors. First, there was the cumulative effect of sixty years of Gladstonian reforms, which, taken as a whole, acquired a semi- mythical dimension in the collective memory of three generations of democratic sympathizers and Liberal voters. Second, there was the fact that, besides being individually important, many of such reforms elicited strong aristocratic opposition, which further boosted Gladstone's reputation as the common people's advocate. Finally, his radical persona benefited from his public image as a commoner, to which he adhered despite the Crown's repeated offers of a peerage. As a contemporary observer pointed out,

> Mr. Gladstone's refusal of the earldom which was so grudgingly offered to him after his recent defeat has still further raised him in the estimation of the majority of his countrymen. He has sprung from the people; he is still of the people; and the people venerate and love him accordingly.[7]

There was no contradiction between his status as a commoner and his actual lifestyle as the squire of Hawarden: not only was there a long tradition of gentlemen-radicals, stretching back to 'Orator Hunt' and beyond; but also many a Nonconformist recognized in Gladstone's stern countenance the features of the Dissenters' greatest political hero, Oliver Cromwell, himself a squire and quintessential country gentleman.

It may be appropriate to conclude with two other contemporary assessments of Gladstone's career, one critical, the other enthusiastic, but both substantially fair. George Brooks commented in 1885:

> During the past five years, at any rate, no Liberalism but that which consists in a belief in Mr Gladstone and an adoption of his principles has been known in the House of Commons.... He has been regarded as the loyal Liberal, and he alone, who followed Mr. Gladstone whithersoever he went.... The great Liberal Party has no creed but Gladstoneism [sic]. This is at once its strength and its weakness.[8]

From a different angle, a radical admirer wrote that Gladstone's great achievement was that

> he found the people who live in cottages hostile to political parties, and ... succeeded in uniting them with the rest of his countrymen. Those who are old enough to remember the sentiments of the working classes thirty or forty [years] ago will not need to be told that they were a nation apart, that they had nothing in common with the political parties of the day, that they were, in fact, at war with every government which came into existence. Well, Mr. Gladstone has remedied this unhappy state of things. Politics now, at all events to a large extent, are of no class. Working men, instead of being a party of themselves, are honourably associated with the great party of progress.[9]

NOTES

1. Cit. in Morley, *The Life of William Ewart Gladstone* (1903), vol. i, p. 168.
2. 'A prophet for the left', *The Economist*, 18–24 April 1992.
3. K. O. Morgan, 'Editor's Foreword' to A. Ramm, *William Ewart Gladstone* (1989), p. ix.

1 The Rising Hope

1. Thomas Gladstones to his son John, 31 March 1787, cit. in S. G. Checkland, *The Gladstones: A Family Biography 1764–1851* (1971), p. 408.
2. Checkland, *The Gladstones*, p. 8.
3. From this point of view he can be regarded as the personification of Max Weber's 'idealtype', as expounded in his famous essay *The Protestant Ethic and the Spirit of Capitalism* (1965).
4. Morley, *Gladstone*, vol. i (1903), p. 23.
5. M. R. D. Foot, *Gladstone Diaries*, vol. i (1968), p. 29.
6. Gladstone in 1831, cit. in H. C. G. Matthew, *Gladstone*, vol. i (1986), p. 34.
7. D. W. Bebbington, *William Ewart Gladstone. Faith and Politics in Victorian Britain* (1993), p. 237.
8. Matthew, *Gladstone Diaries*, vol. xiv (1994), p. 321.
9. J. Brooke and M. Sorenson (eds), *Prime Minister's Papers: Gladstone*, vol. i (1971), p. 36; cf. Foot, *Gladstone Diaries*, vol. i (16 Oct. 1832).
10. In Morley's words, with which Gladstone strongly agreed: Morley/Gladstone dialogues at Biarritz (16 Dec. 1891), in A. Briggs (ed.), *Gladstone's Boswell. Late Victorian Conversations* (1984), p. 197.
11. Matthew, *Gladstone*, vol. i, p. 199.

12. Cit. in C. Cruise O'Brien, 'New Introduction' to M. Arnold (ed.), E. Burke, *Irish Affairs* (London) 1988, p. xiii; cf. E. Burke, 'A Letter from Mr. Burke to a Member of the National Assembly' (1791), in *Reflections on the French Revolution and Other Essays* (Everyman's edition, 1943), pp. 276–8.

13. Morley, *Gladstone*, vol. ii, pp. 240–1.

14. Morley/Gladstone dialogues at Biarritz (16 Dec. 1891), in Briggs (ed.), *Gladstone's Boswell*, p. 201; emphasis in the text.

15. Cit. in Morley, *Gladstone*, vol. i, p. 183.

16. See the memos dated 3 Feb., 29 Apr. and 3 May 1845, in J. Brooke and M. Sorensen (eds), *The Prime Ministers' Papers: W. E. Gladstone*, II: *Autobiographical Memoranda* (1972), pp. 273–9.

17. Checkland, *The Gladstones*, p. 395.

18. The obvious examples are Sir Charles Dilke in 1886 and Charles Stewart Parnell in 1890–91, although it should be observed that in the earlier part of the century Lord Melbourne survived scandal, while Palmerston and Hartington were unscathed by their extra-marital affairs.

19. J. Marlow, *Mr and Mrs Gladstone. An Intimate Biography* (1977), p. 28.

20. Ibid., p. 40.

21. Ibid.

22. Matthew, *Gladstone*, vol. i, p. 242.

23. Checkland, *Mr and Mrs Gladstone*, p. 400.

24. Gladstone to his father in 1838, cit. in Morley, *Gladstone*, vol. i, p. 183.

25. Matthew, *Gladstone*, vol. i, p. 67.

26. Cit. in Morley, *Gladstone*, vol. i, p. 281.

27. Morley, *Gladstone*, vol. i, p. 327.

28. Bebbington, *Gladstone*, p. 171.

29. Cf. Briggs (ed.), *Gladstone's Boswell*, pp. 102, 172.

30. Morley/Gladstone dialogues at Biarritz (27 Dec. 1891), in Briggs (ed.), *Gladstone's Boswell*, p. 202.

31. Cit. in Morley, *Gladstone*, vol. i, p. 363.

2   Free Trade and Financial Reform

1. At first they called themselves Protectionists rather than Conservatives.

2. E. W. Hamilton, *Mr Gladstone: a Monograph* (1898), p. 123.

3. Cf. T. Jenkins, *Disraeli and Victorian Conservatism* (1996), pp. 43–5.

4. Lord Stanley, diary entry for 16 July 1869, in J. Vincent (ed.), Disraeli, *Derby and the Conservative Party. Journals and Memoirs of Edward Henry Lord Stanley, 1841–1869* (1978), p. 341.

5. T. L. Crosby, *The Two Mr. Gladstones. A Study in Psychology and History* (1997), p. 6.

6. W. E. Gladstone, *The Financial Statements of 1853, 1860–1863* (1864), speech of 18 Apr. 1853, p. 53.

7. Though it is difficult to understand how Gladstone could actually hope to continue his policies of free trade and financial reform without the income tax, his strategy is discussed in detail in the final section of Chapter 3.

8. Matthew, *Gladstone*, vol. i, p. 127.

9. Ibid., vol. i, p. 172; see also B. Hilton, *The Age of Atonement. The Influence of Evangelicalism on Social and Economic Thought 1785–1865* (1988), pp. 340–72.

10. Goldwin Smith, *My Memory of Gladstone* (1904), pp. 2–3.

11. In a speech at Manchester on 11 October 1853: cit. in F. W. Hirst, *Gladstone as a Financier and an Economist*, with an introduction by H. N. Gladstone (1931), p. 156.

12. Gladstone, *The Financial Statements of 1853, 1860–1863*, speech of 10 Feb. 1860, pp. 136–7.

13. Ibid., speech of 15 Apr. 1861, pp. 242–3.

14. Cit. in S. Buxton, *Gladstone as Chancellor of the Exchequer* (1901), p. 45; cf. S. Northcote, *Twenty Years of Financial Policy* (1862), p. 69; Matthew, *Gladstone*, vol. i, p. 213.

15. Cit. in Hirst, *Gladstone as a Financier*, p. 186.

16. Gladstone, *The Financial Statements of 1853, 1860–1863*, speech of 10 Feb. 1860, p. 172.

17. E. F. Biagini, *Liberty, Retrenchment and Reform. Popular Liberalism in the Age of Gladstone, 1860–1880* (1992), p. 100.

18. Of course, the practical success of Gladstone's free-trade strategy depended – to a considerable extent – on lucky timing, and particularly on the fact that it was implemented during the boom period between 1850 and 1873.

3 Prime Minister

1. Matthew, *Gladstone*, vol. i, p. 139.

2. The nickname was inspired by the biblical episode of the cave of Adullam, in which discontents against King Saul's regime congregated (1 Samuel 22:1): in 1866–67 the Adullamites were those who rebelled against Russell and Gladstone.

3. In the 1867 Parliamentary debate on the second Reform Bill Disraeli accepted the Radicals' demand for a 'democratic' franchise for the boroughs (which were predominantly Liberal anyway), but avoided any major redistribution of seats, which might have endangered traditional Conservative strongholds in the counties. In the election of 1874 Conservative strength was concentrated in the English counties (where they held 129 seats), though the Liberals lost over forty English urban constituencies. Moreover, and crucially, Gladstone's party lost most of its Irish seats to the Home Rulers (cf. the first section of Chapter 6). For Gladstone's own analysis of the defeat, see his 'Electoral Facts', *Nineteenth Century*, IV (1878), pp. 955–68. Typically, he denied the Radicals' claim that redistribution was the issue, but acknowledged the full extent of the Irish disaster.

4. G. I. T. Machin, 'Disestablishment and democracy, c. 1840–1930', in E. F. Biagini (ed.), *Citizenship and Community. Liberals, Radicals and Collective Identities in the British Isles, 1865–1931* (1996), pp. 120–48.

5. Paradoxically, Gladstone's 1869 position was not inconsistent with his old ultra-Tory views: as he wrote in a private memorandum in 1844, 'the Irish Church ... if maintained at all ... should be exclusively maintained, and if not exclusively maintained, not maintained at all' (memo dated 12 March 1844, in Brooke and Sorensen (eds), *The Prime Ministers' Papers*, p. 248). Since Robert Peel's Maynooth grant had showed that the Church could no longer be 'exclusively maintained', disestablishment was the logical alternative, however long it may have taken Gladstone to accept its political practicability.

6. Smith, *My Memory of Gladstone*, pp. 2–3.

7. Of course, the Church of England ran a majority of the denominational schools. For the context of this debate within the Liberal party see Biagini, *Liberty*, pp. 202–3.

8. E. P. Biagini, 'British Trade Unions and Popular Political Economy, 1860–1880', *The Historical Journal*, 30:4 (1987), pp. 811–40.

9. See A. Briggs, 'Robert Applegarth and the trade unions', *Victorian People*, London, 1990, pp. 174–205.

10. B. Baysinger and R. Tollison, 'Chaining the Leviathan: the case of Gladstonian finance', *History of Political Economy*, 12:2 (1980), pp.

206–13; and C. G. Leathers, 'Gladstonian finance and the Virginia School of public finance', *ibid.*, 18:3 (1986), pp. 515–21.
11. Hirst, *Gladstone as a Financier.*

4 The Charismatic Leader

1. J. Vincent, *The Formation of the British Liberal Party, 1857–68* (1966 and 1972), p. 246.
2. Checkland, *The Gladstones*, p. 402.
3. Ibid., p. 403.
4. Of course the Eastern Question had wider relevance as an imperial issue, as the Ottoman Empire was traditionally perceived as an effective barrier against Russian expansionism. For the Conservative approach to the issue cf. Jenkins, *Disraeli*, pp. 120–6.
5. Hamilton, *Mr Gladstone. A Monograph*, pp. 1–2.
6. W. T. Stead, *1809–1898: Gladstone. A Character Sketch* (1898), pp. 13–15.
7. Cit. in Hamilton, *Mr Gladstone. A Monograph*, p. 11, footnote.
8. Though it must not be forgotten that Gladstone's supporters comprised a broader cross-section of society, including High and 'broad' Churchmen, Roman Catholic, Evangelical Nonconformists, Nonconformists who were neither Evangelical nor 'orthodox' (the Unitarians), and indeed militant secularists – cf. E. Royle, *Radicals, Republicans and Secularists* (1980). On the other hand, it is also important to remember that many Evangelical Anglicans tended to vote Conservative, especially after 1886.
9. Revd R. Heber Newton, as quoted in G. Brooks, *Gladstonian Liberalism: In Idea and In Fact. Being An Account, Historical and Critical of the Second Administration of the Right Hon. W. E. Gladstone, M.P., from April 29th, 1880, to June 25th, 1885* (1885), pp. 24–5.
10. H. C. G. Matthew, 'Gladstone, Rhetoric and Politics', in P. J. Jagger (ed.), *Gladstone* (1998), pp. 235–54.
11. Hamilton, *Mr Gladstone. A Monograph*, pp. 5–6.
12. E.g. Matthew 3:10: 'And now also the axe is laid unto the root of the trees: therefore every tree which bringeth not forth good fruit is hewn down, and cast into the fire.'
13. W. Freer, *My Life's Memories* (1929), pp. 53–4.
14. M. Ostrogorski, *Democracy and the Organization of Political Parties* (1902), vol. ii, p. 308.

15. See Chapter 5.
16. Brooks, *Gladstonian Liberalism*, pp. 23–4. The (?) is in the text. On the power of Gladstone's leadership see P. F. Clarke, *A Question of Leadership. Gladstone to Thatcher* (1991), pp. 11–42.
17. Brooks, *Gladstonian Liberalism*, p. 22.
18. Ibid., pp. 21–2.
19. Ostrogorski, *Democracy*, vol. ii, p. 332.
20. For Parnell's social conservatism and aristocratic outlook cf. L. Kennedy, 'The economic thought of the nation's lost leader', in D. G. Boyce and A. O'Day (eds), *Parnell in Perspective* (1991), pp. 171–200.
21. Cit. in D. M. Schreuder, 'The making of Mr Gladstone's posthumous career: the role of Morley and Knaplund as "Monumental Masons", 1903–27', in B. L. Kinzer (ed.), *The Gladstonian Turn of Mind* (1985), p. 236.
22. Cf. E. F. Biagini, 'Virtue and Victorianism. The Republican Values of British Liberalism, c. 1860–1890', in M. Viroli (ed.), *The Republican Tradition* (forthcoming).
23. J. L. Hammond, *Gladstone and the Irish Nation* (1938), p. 711.
24. T. P. O'Connor, *Gladstone's House of Commons* (1885), entry for 10 March 1883, cit. in C. Silvester, *The Literary Companion to Parliament* (1996), p. 388.

5   Foreign Policy and the Empire

1. *National Expenditure, Speech of the Right Hon. W. E. Gladstone, M.P., in the House of Commons on Mr Ryland's Motion Regarding the Growth of National Expenditure, on Friday, 6th April, 1883*, in *Speeches and Writings*, vol. 8 (1879–85), St Deiniol's Library, Collection of Gladstone's Works, pp. 8–12.
2. *Political Speeches Delivered in Mid-Lothian by the Right Hon. W. E. Gladstone, M.P. (Aug. and Sept. 1884)*, in *Speeches and Writings*, vol. 8, p. 34.
3. Matthew, 'Introduction', *Gladstone Diaries*, vol. x, p. lxvi; see also *Gladstone Diaries*, vol. xi, 'Annotations, letters and Cabinet meetings', March 1885.
4. D. E. D. Beales, 'Gladstone and Garibaldi', in Jagger (ed.), *Gladstone*, pp. 137–56.
5. Briggs (ed.), *Gladstone"s Boswell*, dialogue with L. A. Tollemache (13 Jan. 1896), p. 128.

6. Of course, Belgian neutrality remained a top priority in British foreign policy for the following fifty years: in 1914 it was as a response to the German invasion of Belgium that Britain went to war. In 1939 Belgium, no longer neutral, was still under British (and French) protection.

7. 'Germany, France and England', *Edinburgh Review*, cxxxii (Oct. 1870), pp. 554–93.

8. Hammond, *Gladstone and the Irish Nation*, pp. 698–9.

9. Bebbington, *Gladstone*, p. 179.

10. W. E. Gladstone, *Midlothian Speeches 1879*, with an introduction by M. R. D. Foot (1971), 3rd speech (27 Nov. 1879), p. 128.

11. S.Foerster, W. J. Mommsen and R. Robinson (eds.), *Bismarck, Europe and Africa. The Berlin Africa Conference of 1884–1885 and the Onset of Partition* (1988).

12. W. N. Medlicott, *Bismarck, Gladstone and the Concert of Europe* (1956), p. 337.

13. See above, pp. 75–88.

14. See O. Ralph, *Naoroji. The First Asian MP* (1997), p. 92 ff.

15. Matthew, 'Introduction' to *Gladstone Diaries*, vol. x, p. xc.

16. Gladstone, *Midlothian Speeches 1879* (third speech), pp. 123, 129.

17. Schreuder, 'The making of Mr Gladstone's posthumous career', p. 230.

18. T. R. Metcalf, *Ideologies of the Raj. The New Cambridge History of India*, III.4 (1995), p. 54.

19. For interesting parallels between Jamaica and Ireland in terms of ethnic conflict and the problems involved in granting self-government, see the letter sent by Gordon to Gladstone, 21 January 1882, in 'W. E. Gladstone–A.Hamilton Gordon Correspondence', ed. P. Knaplund, *Transactions of the American Philosophical Society*, new ser., vol. 51, Part 4, 1961, p. 84. For the general methodological and historical context see C. A. Bayly's magisterial *Imperial Meridian. The British Empire and the World 1780–1830* (1989).

6 Ireland

1. R. Brent, *Liberal Anglican Politics* (1987), pp. 65–103.

2. N. Mansergh, *The Irish Question 1840–1921* (1940), pp. 56–82.

3. See Allen Warren, 'Gladstone, land and social reconstruction in Ireland, 1881–1887', *Parliamentary History*, vol. 2 (1983), pp. 153–90.
4. Parnell believed that the Ascendancy class, to whom he belonged, would rejuvenate itself and recover part of its ancient prestige if it joined the national movement and provided leadership for it: see L. Kennedy, 'The economic thought of the nation's lost leader', in Boyce and O'Day (eds), *Parnell in Perspective*, pp. 171–200.
5. J. Shaw, 'Land, people and nation: historicist voices in the Highland land campaign, c. 1850–1883', in Biagini, *Citizenship and Community*, pp. 305–24.
6. Gladstone to Granville, 31 Jan. 1883, in A. Ramm (ed.), *The Political Correspondence of Mr. Gladstone and Lord Granville 1876–1886* (1962, henceforward cit. as *Gladstone–Granville Correspondence*), vol. ii, p. 14.
7. T. A. Jenkins, *Gladstone, Whiggery and the Liberal Party 1874–1886* (1988); J. Parry, *The Rise and Fall of Liberal Government in Victorian Britain* (1993).
8. Cit. in Morley, *Gladstone*, vol. ii, pp. 606–7.
9. Gladstone to Lord Granville, 20 Nov. 1877, in *Gladstone–Granville Correspondence*, vol. i, p. 58.
10. To W. E. Forster, Irish Secretary, 12 Apr. 1882, *Gladstone Diaries*, vol. x, p. 238.
11. Gladstone to Granville, 22 Jan. 1883, in *Gladstone–Granville Correspondence*, vol. ii, p. 11.
12. Ibid. , p. 10.
13. Memo dated 6 May 1883, in *Gladstone–Granville Correspondence*, vol. ii, p. 367.
14. A. B. Cooke and J. Vincent, *The Governing Passion: Cabinet Government and Paty Politics in Britain, 1885–6* (1974).
15. Matthew, *Gladstone*, vol. ii, pp. 188–9, 199–200.
16. *Gladstone Diaries*, vol. x (16 Mar. 1882), p. 103.
17. Gladstone to R. H. Hutton, editor of *The Spectator*, 2 July 1886, in *Gladstone Diaries*, vol. xi, p. 580.
18. Morley, *Gladstone*, vol. i, p. 361.
19. H. C. G. Matthew, 'O'Connell and Gladstone', paper read at the Cambridge Modern Political History Seminar, St John's College, 12 Oct. 1998.
20. See Gladstone's letters to Lord Lorne, 17 Sept. 1885, 'Private', *Gladstone Diaries*, vol. xi, p. 402; and to Lord R. Grosvenor, Chief Whip, 9 Oct. 1885, *ibid.*, p. 411.

21. To the Duke of Argyll, 20 Apr. 1886, *Gladstone Diaries*, vol. xi, p. 535.

22. D. G. Boyce, 'Gladstone and Ireland', in P. J. Jagger (ed.), *Gladstone* (1998), p. 116.

23. Speech on the First Home Rule Bill, 1886, cit. in A. Tinley Bassett (ed.), *Gladstone's Speeches*, London, 1916, pp. 641–2.

24. W. E. Gladstone, *Special Aspects of the Irish Question. A Series of Reflections in and since 1886*, London, 1892, p. 105.

25. Boyce, 'Gladstone and Ireland', p. 108.

26. Warren, 'Gladstone, land and social reconstruction in Ireland, 1881–1887', p. 168.

27. Cit. in ibid. , p. 166.

28. Ibid. , pp. 167–8.

29. Matthew, *Gladstone*, vol. ii, p. 247.

30. Herbert Gladstone, *After Thirty Years* (1928), p. 94, my emphasis.

31. See M. Barker, *Gladstone and Radicalism. The Reconstruction of Liberal Politics in Britain, 1885–1894* (1975).

32. Smith, *My Memory of Gladstone*, p. 71.

33. C. C. O'Brien, *Parnell and His Party 1880–1890* (1957), pp. 193–9; Boyce, 'Gladstone and Ireland', p. 118.

34. M. J. Winstanley, *Gladstone and the Liberal Party* (1990), pp. 62–4.

35. A. B. Cooke and J. Vincent, *The Governing Passion*; a more sophisticated argument is presented in J. Vincent, 'Gladstone and Ireland', *Proceedings of the British Academy*, lxiii (1977), pp. 193–238.

36. J. S. Shepherd, 'Labour and Parliament: the Lib-Labs as the First Working-Class MPs, 1885–1906', in E. F. Biagini and A. J. Reid (eds), *Currents of Radicalism. Popular Radicalism, Organized Labour and Party Politics in Britain, 1850–1914* (1991), p. 198. Cf. report, *The Northern Echo*, 31 May 1886, p. 4, speech by Thomas Burt, MP.

37. 'Ironside', 'The Two Nations', *Newcastle Weekly Chronicle*, 22 Oct. 1881, p. 4.

38. H. Pelling, *Origins of the Labour Party* (1983), pp. 15–18.

39. The SLA embraced Home Rule even before the English National Liberal Federation had made up its mind. Yet, in terms of votes, Home Rule (coupled with the controversial question of disestablishment) turned out to be divisive of the Liberal camp. Overall the Liberal share of the Scottish vote declined from 70 per cent in 1874 to 55 per cent in 1886 (O. and S. Checkland, *Industry and Ethos. Scotland 1832–1914* (1984), p. 84). However, it must be remembered that the 1886 electorate was larger and socially different from the 1874 electorate.

40. The Scottish Liberal Association Papers (SLA), Edinburgh University Library, vol. 40. SLA Meeting and Conference Agendas 1885–91, circular dated October 1887 and signed 'Alex. MacDougall, Secretary'.

41. SLA, Resolutions Adopted at a District Conference of Liberal Associations, 20. x. 1887, Moved by Mr. Wm. Robertson, South Ayrshire; seconded by Mr. J. J. Armistead, Kinbarvie.

42. SLA, Vol. 40, Meeting and Conference Agendas 1885–91, Materials for the preparation of the ANNUAL MEETING OF GENERAL COUNCIL, Edinburgh, 19 February 1889.

43. National Library of Wales, (NLW), T. Gee Papers, 8310 D, 500 a, D. Lloyd George to Miss Gee, 29. 1. 1895.

44. NLW, T. Ellis, 2755, Letter Book, p. 22 (n. d.).

45. NLW, T. Ellis, 4375.

46. NLW, T. Ellis, 3015, Notebook, 2 Sept. 1890.

47. Tom Garvin, *1922. Birth of Irish Democracy* (1996), pp. 152–3.

48. C. Fitzpatrick, 'Nationalising the ideal: Labour and nationalism in Ireland, 1909–1923', in Biagini (ed.), *Citizenship and Community*, pp. 276–304. Cf. Richard English, *Radicals and the Republic. Socialist Republicanism in the Irish Free State 1925–1937* (1994), p. 12: 'The nation, as represented in the 1916 gesture, was not one defined by class conflict but rather one presented in terms of multi-class harmony.'

49. 'Special Article by Mr John Robertson on North East Lanark Election', *Lanarkshire Miners' County Union, Reports and Balance Sheets*, 1904, p. 10 (in Scottish National Library, Edinburgh).

Epilogue

1. Cit. in Schreuder, 'Mr Gladstone's Posthumous Career', p. 236.

2. 'Blair's praise for the Victorian way. Michael White on the PM's not-so-hidden agenda to emulate Gladstone's Liberals', *Guardian*, 16 December 1998, p. 12. As White has pointed out, they have in common that Gladstone was, and Blair is, an Oxford-educated High Churchman with a sense of mission.

3. E.g. Andrew Grice, *Independent*, 2 Jan. 1999, p. 1.

4. Jenkins, *Disraeli*, p. 145.

5. For Moody and Sankey's influence on Gladstone see J. Coffey, 'Democracy and popular religion: Moody and Sankey's mission

to Britain, 1873–5', in Biagini (ed.), *Citizenship and Community*, pp. 93–119.

6. Warren, 'Gladstone, land and social reconstruction in Ireland', pp. 158, 166–7.
7. George Brooks, *Gladstonian Liberalism: In Idea and In Fact. Being An Account, Historical and Critical of the Second Administration of the Right Hon. W. E. Gladstone, M.P., from April 29th, 1880, to June 25th, 1885* (1885), pp. 39–40.
8. Ibid., p. ix.
9. W. E. Adams ('Ironside'), *Newcastle Weekly Chronicle*, 7 Aug. 1880, p. 4.

BIBLIOGRAPHICAL NOTE

The extensive scholarly literature on Gladstone is dominated by two giants: Morley and Matthew. John Morley, *The Life of William Ewart Gladstone* (3 volumes, London, 1903), is a superbly researched work which influenced all those who worked on the topic during the first three-quarters of the twentieth century. For two discussions of Morley's work see M. R. D. Foot, 'Morley's Gladstone: a reappraisal', *Bulletin of the John Rylands Library* (1969), and D. M. Schreuder, 'The making of Mr. Gladstone's posthumous career: the role of Morley and Knaplund as "Monumental Masons", 1903–27', in B. L. Kinzer (ed.), *The Gladstonian Turn of Mind* (1985).

H. C. G. Matthew's monumental edition of the *Gladstone Diaries* (fourteen volumes, 1968–94; vols 1 and 2 edited by M. R. D. Foot) has reshaped the historiographical landscape. The *Diaries* are an extraordinary document, whose full value and potential will be properly appreciated only with the passage of time. With their unparalleled coverage of Victorian politics and culture, they will keep research students and established scholars busy well into the next century. Matthew's two-volume biography of *Gladstone* (1986 and 1996, now available in a one-volume paperback) is by far the subtlest and most thought-provoking recent work – 'a quarry and a classic', to paraphrase Robert Blake.

Other interesting and important biographies are: P. Magnus, *Gladstone: A Biography* (1953); E. J. Feuchtwanger, *Gladstone* (1975); R. Shannon, *Gladstone, vol. 1, 1809–1865* (1982) and *vol. 2, Gladstone Heroic Minister 1865–1898* (1999); T. L. Crosby, *The Two Mr. Gladstones. A Study in Psychology and History* (1997); and, finally, the immensely readable Roy Jenkins, *Gladstone* (1995). P. Stansky, *Gladstone. A Progress in Politics* (1979) and A. Ramm, *Wiliam Ewart Gladstone* (1989) are two elegant and justly acclaimed short studies, the former based on Gladstone's speeches.

On the statesman's family and its influence on his formation see S. G. Checkland, *The Gladstones: A Family Biography 1764–1851* (1971); J. Marlow, *Mr and Mrs Gladstone. An Intimate Biography* (1977); G. Battiscombe, *Mrs Gladstone: Portrait of a Marriage* (1956); and P. Jalland, 'Mr Gladstone's Daughters', in Kinzer (ed.), *The Gladstonian Turn of Mind*.

The religious dimension of Gladstone's life is studied effectively in a series of works, including: A. Ramm, 'Gladstone's religion', *Historical Journal*, xxviii:2 (1985); P. Butler, *Gladstone: Church, State and Tractarianism* (1982); P. J. Jagger, *Gladstone: the Making of a Christian Politician* (1991);

D. W. Bebbington, *William Ewart Gladstone. Faith and Politics in Victorian Britain* (1993); J. Parry, *Democracy and Religion. Gladstone and the Liberal Party 1867–1875* (1986) and B. Hilton, *The Age of Atonement. The Influence of Evangelicalism on Social and Economic Thought 1785–1865* (1988). Religion's relevance for the Liberal party and Gladstone's leadership has been further discussed in Hilton, *Age of Atonement*, and 'Gladstone's theological politics', in M. Bentley and J. Stevenson (eds), *High and Low Politics in Modern Britain* (1983); G. I. T. Machin, 'Gladstone and nonconformity in the 1860's', *Historical Journal*, xvii (1974); and D. W. Bebbington, 'Gladstone and the Non-Conformists: a religious affinity in politics', in *Church, Society and Politics. Studies in Church History* (1975).

Finance and politics are discussed in H. C. G. Matthew, 'Disraeli, Gladstone, and the Politics of Mid-Victorian Budgets', *Historical Journal* (1979); P. Ghosh, 'Disraelian Conservatism: a Financial Approach', *English Historical Review*, xciv (1984); Hilton, *Age of Atonement* and A. Howe, *Free Trade and Liberal England 1846–1946* (1997), especially chapters 4 and 5.

Gladstone's high politics dimension is best studied through R. Shannon, *Gladstone* (1982 and 1999); M. Cowling, *1867. Disraeli, Gladstone and Revolution* (1967); Parry, *Democracy and Religion* and Terry Jenkins, *Gladstone, Whiggery and the Liberal Party, 1874–1886* (1988). Three important collections of essays, covering various aspects of the statesman's career, are: the already mentioned Kinzer (ed.), *The Gladstonian Turn of Mind*; P. J. Jagger (ed.), *Gladstone, Politics and Religion* (1985); and P. J. Jagger (ed.), *Gladstone* (1998).

The Italian Risorgimento played a crucial role in Gladstone's final conversion to liberalism. Various aspects of this development are discussed by D. E. D. Beales, *England and Italy, 1859–1860* (1961); D. M. Schreuder, 'Gladstone and Italian Unification, 1848–70: the making of a Liberal?', *English Historical Review*, 85: 336 (1970); O. Chadwick, 'Young Gladstone and Italy', *Journal of Ecclesiastical History*, xxx (1979); H. C. G. Matthew, 'Gladstone, Vaticanism and the Question of the East', *Studies in Chuch History*, xv (1978), pp. 417–42; and R. Shannon, 'Gladstone, the Roman church and Italy', in M. Bentley (ed.), *Public and Private Doctrine* (1993), pp. 108–26.

For foreign affairs and imperial policy see D. M. Schreuder's book, *Gladstone and Kruger: Liberal Government and Colonial 'Home Rule', 1880–85* (1969) and his article 'Gladstone as a "Troublemaker": Liberal foreign policy and the German annexation of Alsace-Lorraine, 1870–1', *Journal of British Studies*, 17:2 (Spring 1978); see also W. E. Mosse, 'Public opinion and foreign policy: the British public and the war scare of November 1870', *Historical Journal*, 6:1 (1963); K. Sandiford, 'W. E. Gladstone and Liberal-Nationalist Movements', *Albion*, 13:1 (Spring 1981). See also F. Harcourt, 'Gladstone, Monarchism and the "New Imperialism" 1868–1874', *Journal of Imperial and Commonwealth History*, 14 (1985), pp. 20–51; and E. F. Biagini, 'Exporting "Western & Beneficient Institutions": Gladstone and Empire, 1880–85,' in D. Bebbington and R. Swift (eds), *Gladstone Centenary Essays* (2000). Classical studies are P. Knaplund, *Gladstone's Foreign Policy* (1935) and W. N. Medlicott, *Bismarck, Gladstone and the Concert of Europe* (1956); for a more recent study see M. Swartz, *The Politics of British Foreign Policy in the Era of Disraeli and Gladstone* (1985).

On Ireland the classical work remains J. L. Hammond, *Gladstone and the Irish Nation* (1938); for a different, controversial perspective see J. Vincent, 'Gladstone and Ireland', *Proceedings of the British Academy*, 1977, pp. 193–238. Substantial contribution has been offered by A. Warren, 'Gladstone, land and social reconstruction in Ireland, 1881–7', *Parliamentary History*, 2 (1983). However, the most important recent contribution, in this as in most other areas, has been offered by H. C. G. Matthew in both the *Diaries* and the biography.

The popular dimension of Gladstone's liberalism has been investigated by J. Vincent in his classic *The Formation of the British Liberal Party, 1857–68* (1966 and 1972), and, more recently, by E. F. Biagini in *Liberty, Retrenchment and Reform. Popular Liberalism in the Age of Gladstone, 1860–1880* (1992) and P. Joyce, *Visions of the People* (1991), part I. On this topic see also M. Barker, *Gladstone and Radicalism. The Reconstruction of Liberal Politics in Britain, 1885–1894* (1975); and the essays in E. F. Biagini and A. J. Reid (eds), *Currents of Radicalism. Popular Radicalism, Organized Labour and Party Politics in Britain, 1850–1914* (1991); and Biagini (ed.), *Citizenship and Community. Liberals, Radicals and Collective Identities in the British Isles, 1865–1931* (1996). On the Bulgarian Agitation there are two classical studies: R. T. Shannon, *Gladstone and the Bulgarian Agitation, 1876* (1963), and A. Pottinger Saab, *Reluctant Icon. Gladstone, Bulgaria and the Working Classes, 1856–1878* (1991).

Finally, a detailed and extensive bibliography of *Gladstoniana* has been compiled by Ms Lucy M. Adcock, Assistant Librarian of St Deiniol's Library, Hawarden, the Gladstone National Memorial where the statesman's private library and part of his papers are housed. The bibliography can be obtained from the Librarian, St Deiniol's Library, Hawarden, Flintshire CH5 3DF.

CHRONOLOGY

This chronology includes some of the reforms associated with Gladstonian Liberalism and introduced when Gladstone was Prime Minister, though many of them were not initiated by the G.O.M. personally, and in some cases he was suspicious of, if not even hostile to, their implementation. The list is therefore merely indicative and has the aim of providing a general idea of the sort of policies pursued under Gladstone, rather than a precise summary of his policies and achievements.

1809   Born in Liverpool (29 December)
1821–27   Eton College
1828–31   Christ Church, Oxford
1832   Visists Rome; in December elected MP for Newark
1834   Junior Lord of the Treasury
1835   Under-Secretary for War and the Colonies (January); out of office (April)
1838   *The State in Its Relations with the Church*; visits Italy again: Rome, Sicily, Naples
1839   Marries Catherine Glynne
1840   *Church Principles Considered in Their Results*
1841   Vice-President of the Board of Trade: works on revision of tariffs
1843   President of the Board of Trade
1844   Railways Bill
1845   Resigns from Peel Government (January); back in office as Colonial Secretary (December)
1846   Fall of the Peel Government
1847   MP for Oxford University
1850–51   In Naples; *Letters to the Earl of Aberdeen*
1852   Speech on Disraeli's budget (December)
1853   First budget
1854   Crimean War budget (May)
1855   Out of office
1856–58   Advocates 'Christian liberty' (self-determination) for the Danubian Principalities (present-day Romania), then part of the Ottoman Empire
1858   Lord High Commissioner Extraordinary for the Ionian Islands

1859	Chancellor of the Exchequer
1860	Budget and Anglo-French Treaty
1861	Post Office Savings Act
1862	Expresses sympathy for the South in US Civil War; triumphal visit to Newcastle
1863	Speech on the Franchise ('Pale of the Constitution')
1865	MP for South Lancashire; death of Palmerston, Russell Prime Minister
1866	Reform Bill (March); visits Rome (October)
1868	Resolutions for Irish Church Disestablishment (March); MP for Greenwich (November); Prime Minister (December)
1869	Irish Church Disestablishment Act; *Juventus Mundi* (August); Trades Unions' Fund Protection Act; Married Women Property Act
1870	Irish Land Act (February); Elementary Education Act; 'Germany, France and England', anon. in *The Edinburgh Review*
1871	Abolition of Army Purchase by Royal Warrant; Criminal Law Amendment Act (trade unions); Local Government Act; Universities Tests Act
1872	Alabama Claims arbitration; Ballot Act; Licensing Act; Public Health Act
1873	Irish University Bill; the government resigns; back in office (August) as both Prime Minister and Chancellor of the Exchequer
1874	Election defeat (January)
1875	Resigns Liberal party leadership; *Vaticanism*
1876	*The Bulgarian Horrors and the Question of the East* (September)
1877	Speeches on the Eastern Question; inaugural meeting of the National Liberal Federation (NLF)
1878	Attacks Beaconsfield's imperial policy; jingo mob breaks Gladstone's windows
1879	First Midlothian campaign
1880	MP for Midlothian; general election victory; Prime Minister and Chancellor of the Exchequer; Compensation for Disturbances (Ireland) Bill; Burials Act (Nonconformists); Ground Game Act, Employers' Liability Act
1881	Irish Land Act; Boers defeat British troops in Transvaal: Pretoria Convention and 'Home Rule' for Transvaal; Parnell arrested (October); Ilbert Act (India, under Ripon)
1882	May: Parnell released ('Kilmainham Treaty'); Phoenix Park murders; Arrears Act; Coercion Act: July: Alexandria bombarded, invasion of Egypt; India councils (Ripon); December: cedes Exchequer
1883	Corrupt and Illegal Practices Act (against elect. corruption); Agricultural Holdings Act; Cheap Trains Act
1884	Third Reform Act; withdrawal from Sudan, Gen. Gordon to carry out orders

1885	Redistribution Act; death of Gordon at Khartoum; Afghanistan: Pendjeh crisis (with Russia); government, defeated on the budget, resigns (June); contacts with Parnell about Irish government (July); Home Rule plans (November)
1886	Home Rule Bill and Land Reform Bill; election and defeat, following Liberal split
1890	O'Shea divorce and fall of Parnell; *Impregnable Rock of Holy Scripture*
1892	Electoral victory (alliance with Irish National party): Prime Minister; Uganda crisis
1893	Home Rule Bill approved by the Commons, defeated by the Lords; naval scare begins
1894	District and Parish Councils Act; resigns as Prime Minister on increased naval estimates (March); Harcourt's budget includes graduated death duties
1896	Speech on the Armenian massacres
1898	Dies at Hawarden (19 May)

INDEX

Aberdeen, Earl of, 28, 31, 36–7, 57, 79, 115
Afghanistan, 67, 78, 83, 84, 87, 103, 106
Africa, 74, 83, 84, 86–9, 103
America, 13, 44, 59, 60, 63, 66, 69–71, 81, 82, 85, 87, 101, 108, 115–16
Aristotle, 10–1, 13, 71–3
army purchase, 50
Asquith, H. H., 1, 108
Australia, 2
Austrian Empire (Austria-Hungary from 1866), 38, 65, 79–80, 87–8, 102

Ballot Act, 50, 91
Beales, D. E. D., 2
Bebbington, D., 13
Belgium, 79, 80, 81, 123–4
Bismarck, Prince O. von, 2, 69, 81–2, 84–5
Blair, Tony, 66, 114–15, 127
Bradlaugh, C., 56
Bright, John, 48, 49, 59–60, 67, 88
British Empire, 2, 3, 13, 25–6, 53, 82, 85–9, 91, 99, 103–4, 110–11
Bulgarian Agitation, 60–3, 115
Burke, E., 11, 13–14, 25, 44, 85–6, 98, 100–1, 103
Butler, Bishop Joseph, 11–2, 13, 101

Calhoun, John, 116
Calvinism, 4–5, 8–9, 10; see also Church of Scotland, Presbyterians

Cambridge, 19
Canada, 2, 15, 102, 103
Canning, G., 6, 26
Carson, Sir E., 102
Cavour, C., Count of, 38, 79–80, 90
Chamberlain, Joseph, 88, 100, 106, 108, 119
Chartists, 39, 45, 57, 59–60, 110
Checkland, S. G., 7, 58
Chevalier, M., 39
China, 37, 83
Church of England, 5–6, 8, 12, 24, 25, 27, 48, 51, 58, 107–8, 122; see also High Church, Oxford Movement, Tractarians, Evangelicalism
Church of Scotland, 5
Churchill, W. S., 71
class struggle, 72
Clay, Henry, 115–16
Cobden, R., 39, 78–9
Coleridge, S. T., 11
Concert of Europe, 35, 64, 78–85
Conservative party, 37, 46–7, 54–5, 67, 74, 86, 99, 108–9, 112, 121, 122
Corn Laws, 21–4, 41–2, 56, 57; see also free trade, protectionism
Cowling, M., 46
Crimean War, 35, 36, 37, 42, 59
Cromwell, Oliver, 116
Crosby, T., 30–1
Cross, R., 52

Dante, 11–12, 27; see also Italy
Darwin, C., 13–14

135